TESTIFYING ON BEHALF OF CHILDREN

A HANDBOOK FOR CANADIAN PROFESSIONALS

Jessica L. Pratezina

9/13

D1296014

TESTIFYING ON BEHALF OF CHILDREN

A HANDBOOK FOR CANADIAN PROFESSIONALS

ROBIN VOGL

*Former Senior Counsel, Metro Toronto Children's Aid Society,
Toronto, Ontario*

AND

NICHOLAS BALA

Faculty of Law, Queen's University, Kingston, Ontario

THOMPSON EDUCATIONAL PUBLISHING, INC.
Toronto

Copyright (c) 2001 Thompson Educational Publishing, Inc.

Information on how to obtain copies of this book may be obtained from:

Web site: www.thompsonbooks.com
E-mail: publisher@thompsonbooks.com
Telephone: (416) 766-2763
Fax: (416) 766-0398

National Library of Canada Cataloguing in Publication Data

Vogl, Robin
  Testifying on behalf of children : a handbook for Canadian professionals

Includes bibliographical references and index.
ISBN 1-55077-126-4

1. Witnesses - Canada. 2. Evidence, Expert - Canada. 3. Children - Legal status, laws, etc. - Canada. 4. Procedure (Law) - Canada. I. Bala, Nicholas, 1952- . II. Title.

KE9335.V64 2001   347.71'067   C00-933355-X   KF9672.V64
2001

Copy Editing: Elizabeth Phinney
Cover Design: Elan Designs
Reader's Comments: If you have suggestions or information that might improve future editions of this book, the authors and publisher would be pleased to hear from you. Please send your comments to:
author@thompsonbooks.com

We acknowledge the support of the Government of Canada through the Book Publishing Industry Development Program for our publishing activities.

Printed in Canada.

Dedication

This book is dedicated to the memory of the late Dr. Paul D. Steinhauer, a tireless advocate for children in this country.

PREFACE

This book is written for child protection workers, social workers, counsellors, health professionals, teachers and other professionals who work with children. It is intended to provide professionals with a better understanding of our legal system as it relates to the problem of child abuse. It is written by lawyers with extensive experience in the fields of child protection and Family Law. It provides a practical guide to the Canadian legal system, the court process and testifying in court. It is written with particular reference to the legislation of Ontario, but it is useful for professionals throughout Canada.

This handbook is a valuable resource for professionals who are called upon to testify in various proceedings that affect children, especially those involving allegations of the abuse or neglect of children.

This book reflects the law as of January 15, 2001. While it provides useful information for professionals, those with specific legal problems are urged to obtain appropriate legal advice.

ABOUT THE AUTHORS

Robin Vogl, LL.B., graduated in law from Queen's University in 1975. She was Counsel to the Simcoe County Children's Aid Society from 1991-99, and previously worked as Senior Counsel for the Children's Aid Society of Metro Toronto. She assisted in the development of the sexual abuse protocol in Metro Toronto. She also worked previously as a Youth Court Prosecutor and has been a consultant to the Institute for the Prevention of Child Abuse, the Metropolitan Toronto Special Committee on Child Abuse and the Ministry of Community and Social Services. Ms. Vogl has also represented children through both the Ontario Child Representation Program and Justice for Children Legal Aid Clinic. She has also offered training to a wide variety of professionals in the area of child protection and the court process, and co-authored *Canadian Child Welfare Law* (Toronto: Thompson Educational Publishing, 1991).

Nicholas Bala, B.A., LL.B., LL.M., graduated in law from Queen's University in 1977, and received a graduate degree in Law from Harvard in 1980. He has been a Professor at the Faculty of Law, Queen's University, Kingston, Ontario, since 1980, and has also been a visiting professor at McGill, the University of Calgary and Duke Law School in the United States. Professor Bala specializes in Family Law and Children's Law and also teaches Contract Law. He has published extensively about legal issues related to child abuse, divorce and young offenders, including co-authoring *Canadian Child Welfare Law* (Toronto: Thompson Educational Publishing, 1991). He is frequently interviewed by the media, and his work has often been cited by the courts. He has presented to a range of professional audiences and has appeared as a witness at parliamentary committees dealing with legal issues related to families and children.

ACKNOWLEDGEMENTS

We wish to thank Ontario Crown Prosecutor, Elizabeth Quinlan, Peter Dudding of the Child Welfare League of Canada, and Louise Leck of the Ontario Association of Children's Aid Societies, who generously reviewed the manuscript and offered many helpful suggestions. We also wish to acknowledge the assistance of Erin McNamara, Queen's Law 2001, who was hired with the support of grants from the Social Sciences and Humanities Research Council and the Law Faculty at Queen's University.

This handbook is based on an earlier booklet, *Testifying on Behalf of Children: A Handbook for Professionals*. It was written by the same authors and published in two editions in 1989 and 1992 by the Institute for the Prevention of Child Abuse, an important institution that unfortunately no longer exists. The authors also wish to thank the following professionals who reviewed the manuscripts of that booklet: Debbie Cantrell, Ross Dawson, Chris McGoey, Mary Wells, Shirley Lockwood, Ron Luciano, Patricia Sibbald, and Judy Copeland.

TABLE OF CONTENTS

INTRODUCTION

I t can happen to any professional who works with children or families. The call comes, sometimes without much warning, and you are asked to free your schedule for an upcoming court date. The subpoena will be served shortly. Maybe you knew it was coming; maybe you didn't.

This booklet is written primarily for the professional who is called upon to testify in proceedings involving children, especially those in which there are allegations of child abuse or neglect. While police officers and others who are regularly involved in court proceedings may find this material of some use, the following pages are offered specifically as an aid to those who only occasionally enter the world of the courtroom, such as child protection workers, social workers, teachers, doctors and other health care professionals, counsellors, shelter workers, psychologists, daycare, childcare or nursery school personnel or members of the clergy.

When you are called to testify in a case involving a child, you are participating in a process that may have an irreversible impact upon the child's future. By acquiring the knowledge and skills to ensure that you are an effective witness in court, you might help to prevent harm to a child who has already suffered at the hands of an adult, or prevent harm to other children in the future. In some cases, you might help to ensure that the court does not make an inappropriate finding of abuse or neglect.

For most busy professionals, the prospect of testifying in court raises a host of questions and often a considerable amount of anxiety. For those who are not called upon to testify on a regular basis, the foray into the legal world is full of unknowns. It is a forum in which you may find yourself being held accountable for your professional actions and opinions in a very direct way by those not necessarily familiar with the "givens" of your professional orientation. The probing questions and challenges of a lawyer may cause you to re-think some of the comfortable assumptions you hold as a professional or reveal some of the unrecognized biases that are reflected in your perceptions and opinions. Some of the questions you are asked as a witness may seem thoughtless, unnecessary or rude.

Your observations and perceptions as a witness can provide a significant piece of the puzzle that the court must solve to achieve its mandate. The court system is designed to provide a fair process for all those who must live with the outcome. It allows for the presenting and testing of evidence, so the court can see the strengths and weaknesses of the testimony and make a fair and objective decision.

The courtroom is ultimately the site of a unique human drama. The experience can be a smooth, anticlimactic recital of necessary facts, or it can be a highly challenging test of your recollection and professional skills. We cannot predict exactly what your situation will be like. What we can do is to explain some of the main aspects of the process and answer at least some of the questions you might have about testifying. The more you know and understand about the process, the more likely you are to be an effective witness.

The information contained in this handbook is not a substitute for legal advice. We are simply sharing with you our views as to what you may encounter and some tips for making the process a little easier. If you are uncertain about what will happen in court or unsure of your rights and obligations, it would be a good idea for you to consult a lawyer for guidance in your particular situation. You may need to obtain advice about the specific legal issues affecting someone in your profession and how those issues may arise in the context of the case you are involved in. It is especially important to obtain such advice if you are concerned about your obligations or potential liability.

If you are a teacher, getting legal advice may be as easy as picking up the phone to talk with the lawyer who advises your school board. Teachers' unions also usually have access to legal advice. If you are a psychologist or social worker, your provincial professional association may have a lawyer that you may contact for advice or information.

In a child protection or criminal matter, the lawyer for the child protection agency or the Crown Attorney may be able to assist in answering at least some of your questions. Likewise, in a custody and access dispute, the lawyer who is calling you as a witness may be able to provide some helpful information.

You need to appreciate that a lawyer representing a party in the case you are involved in will have an "interest" in the case. In a custody case, for example, a parent's lawyer will contact you because he or she believes that your testimony will assist that parent's case. The Crown Attorney in a criminal case or the child protection agency lawyer in a child protection case is not concerned with "winning" but with ensuring that the evidence is fairly presented in court. However, even if the assistance of one of these lawyers is available, you might still decide to seek independent legal advice elsewhere if you are concerned about specific issues raised by your testifying.

There are many different types of cases in which a professional might be asked to testify. We will focus on the following main types of proceedings directly involving children:

- child protection cases;
- criminal cases involving allegations of child abuse or neglect;
- custody or access hearings involving separated or divorced parents;
- civil tort actions (claims for monetary compensation) involving harm to children;
- cases involving domestic violence.

There are, of course, other cases that affect children, such as prosecutions of young offenders or cases dealing with the commitment of children to mental health facilities. Some of the discussion here will be relevant to those cases as well, but they are not a focus of this handbook.

The first chapter introduces our legal system, and includes some of the basic rules of evidence. It also includes information that we hope will be useful for you if you should be called as a witness in a court hearing.

You may not have the time or need to review all aspects of the legal process. You may find it useful to go directly to the chapters that deal with the questions and issues that most concern you.

CHAPTER 1

THE LEGAL SYSTEM

I n this chapter, we will try to provide you with a basic understanding of some of the principles that form the basis of the court process in Canada, with a special focus on those proceedings that affect children.

THE SOURCES OF LAW

There are four main sources of law in Canada: constitutional law, international law, statute law and the common law.

Constitutional Law

The *Constitution Act* forms the fundamental basis of our legal system. It contains three important components that directly affect the way our legal system works.

1. The Division of Powers between the Federal Government and the Provinces

The *Constitution Act, 1867* divides responsibility for enacting laws between the federal and provincial governments. The list dividing responsibilities was drawn up in 1867, and today, the division of responsibility might seem arbitrary and complex. For some issues, there is a clear division. For example, the responsibility for regulating professionals such as teachers, psychologists and doctors is solely a provincial matter. For many issues affecting children, there is a degree of overlap between the responsibilities of the two levels of government, and some degree of co-operation between the federal and provincial governments is needed to effectively address problems.

criminal laws made by feds, enforced by province

The federal government is given the responsibility for enacting statutes governing criminal law and procedure. However, the provincial government is responsible for the enforcement of the federal criminal law as well as for the administration of justice in the province. The provincial government has responsibility for the civil law (such as tort law that governs damage awards), as well as for most social services, such as health, education and child protection. However, the federal government provides some financial support for social services and promotes some training and policy work in these fields. The *Divorce Act* is a federal statute, but provincial governments have also enacted laws to deal with a range of issues that arise when parents separate.

2. The Establishment of Courts at Different Levels

The federal government is responsible for the appointment of judges to the "superior courts," such as the Ontario Superior Court of Justice and the Alberta Court of Queen's Bench, which, for example, deal with cases under the *Divorce Act*. The provincial governments are responsible for judicial appointments to the "lower courts," such as the Ontario Court of Justice or the Alberta Provincial Court, which are responsible for adoption and child welfare. In some places in Canada, the two levels of government co-operate to make appointments to a "Unified Family Court" that has responsibility for all aspects of family law, including child protection.

3. The Canadian Charter of Rights and Freedoms

The *Charter of Rights* has had a profound influence on our society and legal system. It establishes some important principles that are to be used in the interpretation of all statutes, whether federal or provincial.

This important addition to the Canadian Constitution was introduced in 1982 and guarantees individuals certain rights with regard to their relations with the state and its agencies. For example, section 7 of the *Charter* provides that "everyone has the right to life, liberty and security of the person," and that the individual shall not be deprived of those rights "except in accordance with the principles of fundamental justice." The *Charter* also contains a number of other guaranteed rights, such as protection against unreasonable search or seizure, arbitrary detention or imprisonment, the right to certain information upon arrest, and the right not to be subjected to any cruel or unusual treatment or punishment.

Section 15 of the *Charter of Rights* contains specific guarantees of equal treatment before the law without discrimination based on such grounds as race, religion, gender, age or physical or mental disability. The courts have also held that unjustified discrimination on such grounds as sexual orientation is prohibited, even though these grounds are "unenumerated" (not specifically mentioned) in the *Charter*. The *Charter* provides, however, that the creation of "affirmative action" programs to assist disadvantaged groups is not considered to be "discrimination."

Where a statute is found to be in conflict with a guaranteed right under the *Charter*, the law in question may be ruled unconstitutional and hence without legal effect. Section 1 of the *Charter*, however, offers a "common sense qualifier" by providing that the rights guaranteed by the *Charter* are subject to "such reasonable limits prescribed by law as can be demonstrably justified in a free and democratic society." This gives our courts the authority to determine when a violation of our *Charter* rights is tolerable because it is socially necessary. For example, in some situations discrimination on the basis of age may be justified in order to allow for mandatory retirement at age 65, or to prohibit voting for those under 18 years of age.

The *Charter* allows a government to enact a law that is valid notwithstanding the fact that it violates the *Charter* provided that there is an explicit statement that the government intends to do so. Such a provision will automatically terminate after five years and must be specifically renewed if the override is to continue. The use of the "notwithstanding clause," as it is referred to, is controversial, and governments are very reluctant to use the override provision of the *Charter* unless there are compelling reasons to do so.

In a criminal matter, if a right guaranteed by the *Charter* has been violated in the investigation or prosecution of the case, it might be a basis for "staying" or discontinuing the proceeding against the accused even if he or she is in fact guilty. It may also be used by a court to exclude a particular piece of evidence obtained in violation of the *Charter* if its admission "would bring the administration of justice into disrepute."[1] The exclusion of critical evidence obtained in violation of *Charter* rights may result in the acquittal of a guilty person.

The *Charter of Rights* has been most frequently applied in criminal cases. To date, the *Charter* has had only a limited impact on family disputes and child protection cases, but the courts have clearly recognized that familial relationships are of fundamental importance to individuals and are entitled to constitutional protection. The courts have, for example, held that prohibiting adoption by same-sex partners violates the *Charter* and allowed such couples to adopt a child, if this is in the best interests of the child.

In an important 1999 decision, *New Brunswick* v. *G.(J.),* the Supreme Court recognized that child protection proceedings are a intrusive form of state intervention and a threat to the "liberty and security of the person" of parents and children.[2] Accordingly, under section 7 of the *Charter,* such proceedings are to be conducted "in accordance with the principles of fundamental justice." This will normally require that the state pay for the lawyer for an indigent parent involved in a child protection proceeding, in order to ensure that it is a fair hearing. However, the Supreme Court has also recognized the risk that children

---

[1] *Canadian Charter of Rights and Freedoms,* s. 24(2). Section 24 in its entirety reads as follows:

24. (1) Anyone whose rights or freedoms, as guaranteed by this Charter, have been infringed or denied may apply to a court of competent jurisdiction to obtain such remedy as the court considers appropriate and just in the circumstances.

(2) Where, in proceedings under subsection (1), a court concludes that evidence was obtained in a manner that infringed or denied any rights or freedoms guaranteed by this Charter, the evidence shall be excluded if it is established that, having regard to all the circumstances, the admission of it in the proceedings would bring the administration of justice into disrepute.

[2] [1999] 3 S.C.R. 46. Supreme Court of Canada decisions since 1985 are available on a free website: http://www.lexum.umontreal.ca/csc-scc/en/index.html. A number of other courts, such as the Ontario Court of Appeal, also have free websites, but most judicial decisions are only available through commercial online services such as Quicklaw or in law reports that can be found in law libraries.

might face from abuse and neglect and has upheld the validity of Manitoba legislation that allows child protection agency workers to apprehend a child without prior court authorization, even though this can be a highly intrusive state act.[3]

If a party to a proceeding raises a *Charter* issue, it will usually result in a more complex and delayed court process. As an example, in one case, the definition of "parent" contained in the adoption portion of Ontario's *Child and Family Services Act* was challenged as a possible violation of a biological father's rights to equal treatment under the law. The adoptive family was forced to wait many months for a resolution of the issue in the higher courts, even though it was ultimately held that the father's rights were not violated.

International Law

Canada has signed and ratified a number of international treaties that affect our legal system. For example, the *Hague Conventions* deal with some of the problems that arise when a child is abducted from one country to another and that regulate international adoption. Canada is also a signatory to the *United Nations Convention on the Rights of the Child*, which requires states to promote the interests of children. The *Convention* is a vague document and the primary method of enforcement is through monitoring and political pressure. The Canadian courts have, however, occasionally invoked the *Convention* to protect the interests of children. For example, in one case, the Supreme Court of Canada held that immigration authorities violated the *Convention* by failing to give any consideration to the interests of children who were born in Canada and were Canadian citizens when deciding whether to deport their mother, who had illegally resided in Canada for over a decade.[4]

---

[3] *Winnipeg Child and Family Services* v. *K.L.W.*, 2000 **SCC** 48.

[4] *Baker* v. *Canada*, [1999] 2 S.C.R. 817.

Statute Law

In practice, perhaps the most important source of laws affecting children in Canada are statutes (or legislation) enacted by the federal Parliament and provincial (and territorial) legislatures. As discussed above, under the *Constitution Act, 1867* each level of government has the responsibility to enact laws in their respective area of jurisdiction. The resulting legislation, so long as it does not extend beyond the power of its legislators and does not offend the *Charter*, is valid. The *Criminal Code*, for example, is a piece of federal legislation and therefore binds everyone across Canada. Ontario's *Child and Family Services Act* applies only within Ontario, although there is similar legislation dealing with child protection in other provinces.

Sometimes a legislature will pass different statutes that appear to be in some way inconsistent with each other. If the legislature intends to make an exception to other laws it has enacted, it can use specific wording to make it dear that an exception is intended. As an example, in the professional reporting duties under Ontario's *Child and Family Services Act*, subsection (1) of section 72 begins with the following phrase:

> *Despite the provisions of any other Act*, if a person, including a person who performs professional or official duties with respect to children, has reasonable grounds to suspect one of the following, the person shall forthwith report the suspicion and the information on which it is based to a society....

With these words, the Ontario legislature has made clear its intention to override any of its own legislation that might in some way conflict with the wording of that particular provision. In this example, the use of the specific wording quoted above means that other Ontario legislation which imposes a duty of confidentiality upon professionals does not cancel or eliminate the duty to report child protection concerns.

A province may also enact legislation that is apparently in conflict or inconsistent with federal legislation. When that happens, the courts must decide which statute should prevail. They must refer back to the original division of powers under the *Constitution*

Act to determine which government has the jurisdiction to enact laws in that specific area.

Interpreting Statutes

Legislation is intended to provide direction to courts and citizens. Often a piece of legislation will include some definitions in order to clarify its meaning, although there are frequently situations in which the meaning of a statute is not entirely clear. Most jurisdictions have enacted statutes that offer some assistance to commonly used statutory terms, for example, Ontario's *Interpretation Act*. Such a statute might offer guidance as to how an appeal period is calculated.

In many instances, however, the question of a statute's meaning will be brought before a court, and the court will be asked to make a ruling on the issue. The 1988 amendments to the *Criminal Code of Canada* (Bill C-15) relating to sexual offences against children include the term *"touching for a sexual purpose"* in several of the provisions. The legislation itself does not define the term *"for a sexual purpose."* A decision of the Supreme Court of Canada, however, in a case involving a charge of sexual assault, interpreted a similar term, *"of a sexual nature."* That decision, *R. v. Chase,* has been of assistance to the courts in interpreting the phrase contained in the 1988 provisions.[5]

In *R. v. Chase,* the Supreme Court of Canada held that the test to be applied in determining whether the act has the necessary "sexual" nature is an objective one. The question to be asked is: "Viewed in the light of all circumstances, is the sexual or carnal context of the assault visible to a reasonable observer?" The case also tells us that a court must also consider whether the "sexual integrity" of the victim has been violated and whether or not the motive for the touching was sexual gratification. As can be seen from this example, the words of a statute gain texture and refined meaning when interpreted in the context of a real fact situation before a judge.

---

[5]   *R. v. Chase,* [1987] 2 S.C.R. 293.

Common Law

The term *common law* derives from the English Courts established in the Middle Ages to apply a uniform law common to all of England. The common law consists of law that has been expressed in prior judicial decisions on the issues in question. Some parts of our law, such as contract law, are largely based on common law. The law of evidence, which governs what types of testimony and documents are admissible in court, is also based on the common law, though in recent years there have been significant statutory amendments to the law of evidence. A statute, being the act of the elected legislature, can override the common law, which has been developed by appointed judges.

Legal Precedents and Binding Decisions

Most people are familiar with the concept of precedent in the legal system. This refers to a body of prior decisions that supports a certain approach to a legal issue. Our legal system has also inherited the tradition of *stare decisis* (from the Latin "the decision stands"), which means "to abide by or adhere to, decided cases."

The principle of *stare decisis* means that, when a point of law has been settled by a court decision, it should be adhered to in similar situations by courts of equal or lower rank. It is for this reason that a decision made by a higher court (e.g., the Ontario Court of Appeal) has more legal impact than a decision of a lower court (e.g., the Ontario Court of Justice).

In every province there is a Court of Appeal that makes decisions binding within that province. The Supreme Court of Canada deals with appeals from across the country. Its decisions are binding on all other courts, unless they involve the interpretation of a provincial statute. The Supreme Court deals with only about one hundred cases a year. It is expensive and time consuming to appeal to this level of court, and access to full hearings is restricted by a screening process known as "seeking leave to appeal." In this process, a panel of three judges review documents and hold a summary hearing to determine whether a case is of "national importance" and merits a full hearing.

THE COURT STRUCTURE

Most Canadian provinces have a complex court structure. In some provinces, such as Ontario, frequent changes in name and jurisdiction, and variation within the province, add to the complexity.

In each province there is a "superior court" with judges appointed by the federal government. In Ontario, this is the Superior Court of Justice, and in Alberta, it is called the Court of Queen's Bench. This level of court deals with divorce, major civil cases and the most serious criminal cases. Jury trials can only be conducted in superior court.

In each province, there is a level of court with funding and judicial appointments from the provincial government. In Ontario, this is now called the Ontario Court of Justice. These courts are sometimes referred to as "provincial courts," or by the unfortunate technical term *inferior courts* (as distinguished from the "superior courts"). In practice, these courts deal with a relatively large number of cases, often in a less formal and more expeditious fashion than the superior courts. The provincial courts have jurisdiction over many criminal cases, including almost all young offenders cases, adoption and child welfare and some proceedings relating to parental separation, as well as enforcement of all support orders. In some provinces, there is an administrative division within the provincial court between a criminal and a family division. There is a Small Claims Court, or civil division of the provincial court, which, in Ontario for example, generally deals with claims of up to $10,000.

Unified Family Courts

In the area of family and children's law, some issues have traditionally been dealt with in the provincial courts, but not all. Child protection, adoption and enforcement of support orders are dealt with in the provincial court. However, if property needs to be divided or if a divorce is sought, only a superior court is empowered to deal with these issues. Some issues can be dealt with in either level of court, such as support, custody and access.

Increasingly in Canada, the courts are being "unified" so that one court has jurisdiction to deal with all aspects of family law. In some places this is referred to as the "Unified Family Court." In Ontario, a number of locales have a Unified Family Court (called simply the "Family Court"), while other locales continue to have two levels of court dealing with family law issues. A common feature of Unified Family Courts is the availability of a range of support services located at the court, such as mediation and family law information centres, which provide brochures and assistance to the public.

KINDS OF LEGAL PROCEEDINGS

There are a number of different kinds of legal proceedings. These proceedings can have different functions and take place in different courts under different rules of evidence and procedure.

It is, for example, possible for a number of different kinds of proceedings to arise out of a single incident of child abuse or neglect. If a doctor is alleged to have abused a child patient, he might be charged with sexual assault under the *Criminal Code.* The child protection agency might also investigate and find that he is potentially a high risk to his own children and take steps to bring those children before the court as children "in need of protection." Likewise, the child protection agency might take steps to place his name on a register for child abusers, if one existed in that province. In addition, he would likely face disciplinary proceedings by the College of Physicians and Surgeons. He might also be sued in civil proceedings on the child victim's behalf for monetary damages sustained as a result of the abuse.

As you can see, a single incident of abuse could give rise to a number of distinct proceedings. Generally, court proceedings are divided into two categories: criminal and civil.

Criminal Proceedings

Criminal proceedings are those proceedings that arise out of alleged violations of the *Criminal Code.* There are also offences found in other pieces of legislation besides the *Criminal Code,* such as the *Controlled Drugs and Substances Act.* Where someone is found guilty of an offence, whether found in the *Criminal Code* or elsewhere, he or she is liable for punishment.

An example of an offence relating to child abuse that is not contained in the *Criminal Code* would be the offence contained in subsection 79(2) of Ontario's *Child and Family Services Act*, which provides:

> No person having charge of a child shall,
>
> > *(a)* inflict abuse on the child; or
> >
> > *(b)* by failing to care and provide for or supervise and protect the child adequately,
> >
> > > (i) permit the child to suffer abuse, or
> > >
> > > (ii) permit the child to suffer from a mental, emotional or developmental condition that if not remedied, could seriously impair the child's development.

Subsection 85(2) of the Ontario *Child and Family Services Act* provides for a potential fine of up to $2,000 or imprisonment of up to two years or both for an individual who is found guilty of this offence.

Proceedings involving offences are set apart from civil proceedings for understandable reasons. Because the accused faces prosecution by the state with the possibility of incarceration, the law provides a considerable measure of protection for the individual accused.

A significant aspect of a criminal prosecution is that the burden is on the Crown to prove its case "*beyond a reasonable doubt.*" This high standard means that suspicion or probability of guilt is not enough to allow a conviction. Any reasonable doubt must be resolved in favour of the accused. The notion that underlies this onus upon the state to prove guilt has its roots in the ancient common law maxim: "Better ninety-nine guilty persons go free, than for one innocent person to be convicted." However, it is also said that the Crown does not have to provide "absolute certainty" of guilt, and that the accused should not be acquitted based on sympathy or a frivolous doubt.

In an attempt to ensure the fairness of criminal proceedings, the rules of evidence are relatively strict. For example, a child will often be spared from having to testify in a civil custody dispute between parents. However, if an allegation of abuse is made in a criminal context, it will normally be necessary for the child to testify unless the child is considered too young to be able to do so. (See page 73, "The Rules of Evidence.") The *Charter of Rights* also provides an accused person with an array of protections throughout the criminal process.

Another characteristic of criminal court is its public nature. Traditionally, criminal proceedings were open to the public to observe so that the accused was not vulnerable to a "secret" process. That tradition has continued so that the public will rarely be asked to leave a criminal courtroom, although the judge has the power to exclude the public in limited circumstances. To do so, a court must find that "the proper administration of justice requires" the public to be excluded. It is relatively rare for such an order to be made. It is not uncommon, however, for a judge to ban publication in criminal matters, particularly where sexual offences against children are involved. It is also not uncommon for a court to order that a young child victim may testify from behind a screen or via closed-circuit television, where available and appropriate, though it is often necessary for the Crown Attorney to call professional evidence supporting such an application. Child witnesses may be permitted to bring "support persons" to court, so long as the support person is not a witness in the proceedings.

Sometimes, in offences involving child abuse, the Crown Attorney will deal with the case after all the others to ensure that the courtroom is as private as possible, without the necessity of an order excluding the public.

While civil trials are almost always decided by a judge alone, in more serious criminal cases, the accused has a choice (or "election") to have a jury trial.

Victim Witness Programs

In many localities there are programs to assist victims and other witnesses who are testifying in criminal proceedings. Workers can provide information about the court process and emotional support for vulnerable witnesses, in particular, children and abused women. Victim witness workers liaise with police and the Crown Attorney and will often attend court with vulnerable witnesses. Contact your local Crown Attorney's office for information.

Commencing the Criminal Process

Where there is suspicion of an offence having occurred, perhaps based on a report from the community, the police will investigate and must decide if there are reasonable grounds to believe that a criminal offence has been committed. In such cases, criminal charges may be laid. Technically, charges are commenced by the police appearing before a Justice of the Peace (a lower level of judge, often without formal legal training) to "swear an information," i.e., make a sworn statement that they have reasonable grounds to believe that an offence has occurred. Criminal charges are laid in the place where the offence is alleged to have occurred, which may not be where the victim or offender resides.

In theory, police are not the only persons who can lay charges. Private citizens have the right to make an appointment with a Justice of the Peace and to lay charges, so long as they can satisfy a Justice of the Peace that there are reasonable grounds to believe that an offence has been committed. In most places, the Crown Attorney will still conduct the prosecution even if a citizen lays charges.

Typically, in the course of an investigation, or soon after the accused is arrested, the police will want to question the suspect. In Canada, the *Charter of Rights* guarantees the right to silence, though many people who are suspected of offences want the police to hear "their side of the story." Accused persons have the right to consult with a lawyer as soon as they are arrested. If the rights of an accused person are not respected after arrest, the courts are likely to rule that any statement that is obtained is inadmissible in any court proceedings. There are legal aid programs in all provinces in Canada, and an accused with limited financial resources may be eligible for a lawyer paid by the government-funded legal aid plan.

Before a case goes to trial, there must be "disclosure" to the accused by the Crown of the evidence gathered by the police. This will usually be done by a Crown Attorney at a meeting with defence counsel. Some information collected by the police may be considered "privileged" and protected from disclosure. In some cases the police may have access to highly personal counselling records related to a victim. A judge may have to decide whether sensitive material should be disclosed to the defence, balancing the right of the accused to a fair trial against the privacy interests of the victim.[6]

The Crown Attorney will also "screen" the file before it goes to trial, and may decide that charges should be dropped because there is not a reasonable likelihood of conviction. Or the Crown may consider that the charges would be better dealt with outside the formal court system and refer the case to some form of diversion or alternative measures program. Diversion is most common with less serious charges and cases involving young offenders.

Release Pending Trial

If an accused has been arrested, he or she is often released by the police on an *Undertaking to Appear* or pursuant to a *Recognizance.* The accused is required to appear in court on a specific date, and may be subject to certain conditions of release, such as abstaining from communicating with an alleged victim or witness.

If the charge is serious, such as sexual assault of a child, the accused may be detained in jail. Persons who are detained by the police must be brought before a Justice of the Peace within 24 hours for a "bail hearing" (technically called a judicial interim release hearing). In many cases, the Crown Attorney will agree that the court should release the accused on certain conditions. For example, in the case of someone charged with "sexual interference" involving a young female child, the conditions might prohibit him from having any contact with females under the age of 16. In a case involving father-daughter incest, the Crown

---

[6] See the *Criminal Code,* s 278.1 to 278.9 and *R.* v. *Mills,* [1999] 3 S.C.R. 668. See discussion p.84-85.

Attorney might insist that there be a condition attached to the release prohibiting any contact by the accused with his family and that the accused reside outside the home.

In some cases, especially where the accused has a record of non-attendance at previous court dates, or the accused has a criminal record and the allegations are serious, the judge may order that the accused be detained in custody while awaiting trial. Where the accused is held in custody awaiting trial, the court will usually attempt to give the case priority in scheduling a trial.

The Kinds of Offences: Summary Conviction, Hybrid, Indictable

Summary conviction offences are those considered to be less serious, and generally have a maximum penalty attached of $2,000 and either 6 months or 18 months imprisonment, depending on the charge. Summary proceedings occur before a provincial court judge with no option for a jury.

Most criminal offences relating to the abuse of children are *hybrid* offences. This means that the Crown Attorney may choose one of two ways to proceed: by way of "summary conviction" or by way of "indictment." The decision to proceed by summary conviction or by indictment depends on a number of factors. Some of the considerations are the seriousness of the allegations, whether the offence was committed within the last six months (if not, the Crown must proceed by way of indictment), the prior criminal record of the accused, the effects of a potentially lengthier proceeding (indictable) upon the victim and the range of sentencing available. Sometimes an accused will be prepared to plead guilty to an offence provided that the case proceeds as a summary conviction offence with more limited penalties. If the offence was a single incident and the accused has no criminal record, the Crown Attorney might be prepared to proceed by way of summary conviction, particularly where the accused agrees to plead guilty, and the child can avoid testifying.

In many child abuse cases, however, the Crown Attorney decides that the circumstances warrant proceeding by way of *indictment.* Because the range of penalties is potentially much more severe for indictable offences than for summary conviction offences, the accused is given greater protection in the process.

For indictable offences, there is usually a preliminary inquiry in the provincial court to determine if there is sufficient evidence to warrant a trial of the accused. The preliminary inquiry (or preliminary hearing) allows the defence counsel to hear the kind of evidence that the Crown has against the accused. Occasionally, an accused will be discharged at the preliminary inquiry stage. In these cases, the judge decides that there is insufficient evidence to warrant having the accused face a trial.

Many Crown Attorneys call a minimum of evidence at a preliminary inquiry. It is unusual for a professional involved with a child, such as a doctor or social worker, to be requested to attend at the preliminary stage, although the alleged victim (technically referred to as the "complainant") will likely have to testify.

In most cases, a person charged with an indictable offence has a choice: to be tried before a judge at the provincial level or to be tried by a superior court judge, with or without a jury. This choice, referred to as an "election," is usually made by the accused with the assistance of a lawyer.

Adjournments

Adjournments are also very common. In the early stages of a criminal proceeding, the accused may be asking for time to obtain legal aid or to retain counsel. Frequently, counsel for the accused will ask for time to obtain Crown disclosure or to carry out its own investigation about the alleged offence.

In the case of indictable offences, there must usually be a preliminary inquiry. If a preliminary inquiry is held, and the judge finds that there is evidence warranting a trial, then a trial date will be scheduled immediately following the preliminary inquiry, to take place often many months later. In cases where a preliminary inquiry is not required, a trial date will be set earlier in the process.

Professionals are not generally required to attend these initial court appearances. If you are required for some reason to attend one of these initial appearances, you will probably be contacted by the Crown Attorney or defence counsel, who will explain why your attendance is necessary. Most professionals who are asked to testify are served with a subpoena by the party requesting their attendance at court.

While there are often several adjournments prior to the setting of a trial date, it is less common for a trial itself to be adjourned because so many people will be inconvenienced by the postponement. The absence of a report or a witness may justify a request that a trial be postponed. In most cases, the lawyers will advise each other beforehand about the need for an adjournment of a trial date so that witnesses are not needlessly inconvenienced. When the adjournment is opposed by one of the parties, however, the witnesses will need to be available in case the request for an adjournment is denied by the court.

Trials

Trials frequently span several days. Since the time to complete the testimony of any one witness is very difficult to predict, it may be necessary for a witness to re-attend on a future day to begin or complete his or her testimony.

A professional who had worked with a child might be called upon to give the following kinds of evidence in a criminal trial:

- a detailed description of the interview with the child when disclosure took place;
- if you have been involved in the making of a video or audio tape, you might be asked to testify concerning: the circumstances surrounding the making of the tape; the security of the tape after it was made; any pauses in the interview (e.g., breaks) (see page 87, "Video and Audiotapes");
- statements made to the professional by a child soon after the alleged incident may be admitted (see "Hearsay," page 78);
- injuries or other evidence of abuse observed by the professional.

A person qualified as an "expert" and permitted to give "opinion evidence" (see page 85) may be asked:

- whether a child is competent to testify;
- whether it is necessary to use a screen or closed-circuit television in order to permit the child to testify;
- about characteristics of abused children;
- about children's disclosure patterns;
- about relevant research or theoretical concepts, such as a physician being asked about battered child syndrome;
- to comment on a hypothetical fact situation (i.e., comment upon a situation that is described in detail to the witness);
- about medical findings that are corroborative of the fact of abuse, i.e., physical evidence of abuse.

Once an accused has been found guilty, a professional witness may be asked to present evidence at the sentencing hearing about

- the impact of the abuse upon the child;
- the impact of the trial process upon the child;
- the relationship between the child and the perpetrator;
- treatment issues regarding the accused.

Sentencing

An accused person who is acquitted will be released without punishment. If found guilty, the accused may face a range of sentences up to and including, in the case of indictable offences, a lengthy prison term. Most often, the sentencing will take place on a date following the finding of guilt. At the sentencing hearing, the Crown Attorney and defence lawyer may call witnesses or file reports regarding the kind of sentence that would be appropriate for the defendant. The judge may ask for a pre-sentence report to be prepared by a probation officer prior to sentencing, containing a social history of the defendant and perhaps recommendations regarding sentencing.

The Crown Attorney may submit to the court a "Victim Impact Statement" summarizing the effect of the offence upon the victim. A professional may sometimes be called upon to provide information for a Victim Impact Statement. In some cases, a professional may even assist in the completion of the statement itself. It is preferable for the Victim Impact Statement to be completed *after* the accused is found guilty. If it is completed before conviction, the child may be cross-examined on its contents during the trial. The statement, if submitted, will be considered by the court in the sentencing process.

There has been considerable concern expressed by some advocates for children about the relative leniency of sentencing in child abuse cases and the apparent lack of judicial awareness of the profound long-term consequences of abuse for children, even in the absence of physical violence. With increased judicial education and public pressure, a trend towards longer sentences in child abuse and domestic violence cases has been apparent in recent years, although critics continue to question the adequacy of current sentencing practices.

In the case of child sexual abuse, the range of sentencing could be from an order of probation with a treatment condition (for example, in a case involving a single incident of sexual touching of a child) to an order of several years' imprisonment (for a offender convicted of having sexual intercourse over an extended period of time with a child who is dependent upon him).

Plea Discussions (or "Plea Bargaining")

Frequently, the defence lawyer and the Crown Attorney will have "plea discussions" to determine whether they can agree to a reasonable disposition of a criminal case without the necessity of a trial. The Crown Attorney, in determining what disposition of a case is appropriate, must assess its strengths and weaknesses, the public interest and the effect of having to testify upon the victim. A plea of guilty is generally considered to be a "mitigating" or positive factor in sentencing. There may be an agreement between counsel as to a term of imprisonment for a particular period. Technically, the judge is not bound to accept the agreement of the lawyers, but as a rule the agreed upon terms are adopted by the courts as an efficient means of disposing of a large number of cases within the system.

Plea discussions can take place at any time in the proceedings and might result in a last-minute agreement just before or on the trial date. If this occurs, witnesses who have been summonsed are usually released from their duty to appear by the investigating officer or Crown Attorney.

Some Crown Attorneys consult with the police and the victim before deciding whether to enter into a plea bargain, but there is no obligation to do so.

Criminal Law Enforcement

In Ontario, the responsibility for the enforcement of criminal law is divided among three police forces: the Royal Canadian Mounted Police (R.C.M.P.), the Ontario Provincial Police (O.P.P.) and municipal police forces.

The Royal Canadian Mounted Police: The R.C.M.P. are appointed under the authority of federal legislation and are responsible to the Solicitor General of Canada. They perform a variety of police duties, particularly in the areas of drug enforcement and national security. In eight provinces the government has agreed to have the R.C.M.P. perform provincial police duties, including investigations of child abuse.

Provincial police: In Ontario and Quebec, there are provincial police forces that are responsible for the investigation of violations of the federal criminal law and provincial legislation occurring outside of major municipalities that have their own police forces. The provincial police are responsible for child abuse cases within the areas in which they provide police services.

Municipal police forces: Many Canadian cities have their own municipal police forces accountable to the local police commission. These officers are responsible for the investigation of violations of the *Criminal Code*, provincial legislation and city by-laws taking place within the boundaries of the municipal region. Municipal police typically handle child abuse investigations. In cities and towns without municipal forces, police work is performed by the provincial police or R.C.M.P.

Civil Proceedings

The term *civil proceedings* refers to all proceedings that do not involve prosecution for criminal offences. Examples would include child protection proceedings, divorce, custody and access disputes, breach of contracts, tort actions for recovery of monetary damages, and professional discipline proceedings. Civil cases might involve litigation between a government agency and an individual. An example would be a case in which a child protection agency is seeking permanent custody of a child. A civil matter could also involve litigation between individuals in which no government agency is involved, such as a dispute between parents over custody.

Those who are asking a court to make a civil finding must establish proof "*on the balance of probabilities.*" This test conjures up images of the traditional scales of justice, tipped, even if only by a slight margin, in favour of one side. Some people describe the test as 51 percent certainty, as opposed to the higher criminal standard of proof *beyond a reasonable doubt.*

There are civil cases, such as those involving child protection, in which a central issue may be conduct that would also constitute an alleged criminal act, such as child abuse. It is not uncommon, especially when the alleged abuse takes place within the family, for criminal proceedings to be going on at the same time as a child protection proceeding or a custody dispute between parents. In some cases, there may not be sufficient evidence to result in a criminal conviction. However, in the civil proceeding, the judge may be satisfied that a child has suffered abuse in deciding whether a child is in need of protection or whether a parent should be denied custody or access. This difference reflects the fact that proceedings not directly involving criminal charges have, generally speaking, a lower standard of proof, less strict rules of evidence and fewer *Charter* issues.

Child Protection Agencies

Child welfare or protection functions are carried out in different ways depending upon the province. In some provinces, such as British Columbia, the government is directly responsible for

Civil proceedings are not about punishment.

protecting children. In Ontario, there are 54 separate non-profit corporations providing child protection services (sometimes referred to as Children's Aid Societies or as Child and Family Services) as well as some First Nations child protection services. Each of these organizations receives funding from the province and is regulated by statute, regulations and standards. Each has its own board of directors and is responsible for carrying out child protection responsibilities for children within its geographical boundaries. A few of the Ontario agencies serve members of particular religious groups (Catholic or Jewish), or only serve aboriginal children, but most serve all children and families within a specific jurisdiction.

Child Protection Proceedings

Child protection proceedings are characterized as civil proceedings because they do not have the punishment of parents as their objective, but rather the protection of children. They do, however, resemble in some ways the dynamics of a criminal prosecution in that the applicant is a government-funded agency. When the application is for permanent custody of a child and termination of parental rights, the consequences may be more serious than in the criminal court. Accordingly, some judges may in practice regard the standard of proof in child protection cases as somewhat higher than in ordinary civil cases, though, in theory, the standard of proof is the ordinary civil standard of proof on the balance of probabilities.

Further, it is now accepted that the *Charter of Rights* applies to child protection hearings, requiring that the proceedings are conducted "in accordance with the principles of fundamental justice." Thus, low-income parents are generally entitled to have counsel provided by the state, and the agency is obliged to disclose to counsel for the parents the evidence that it plans to call at trial so that there can be a full and fair hearing.

Each province has its own legislation for the protection of children. Usually the child protection agency must prove certain facts to justify a "finding" of the need for protection in order to allow a court to make a supervision, temporary (or Society) wardship or permanent (or Crown) wardship order.

A supervision order permits a child protection agency to visit the home on a regular basis. A judge may attach conditions to a supervision order, clarifying the expectations of the parent (e.g., treatment for substance abuse).

Sometimes it is necessary to keep a child in foster care for a period of time to allow parents to ready themselves for full-time custody of the child. In this case, temporary wardship is ordered. When a child is ordered a temporary ward, the judge usually makes an order allowing visits between the parent and child, sometimes on a supervised basis, where there is evidence of risk to the child. In extreme cases, access or visiting will be suspended, particularly if a child does not wish to see the parent.

Where a child is unable to live with his or her family for the foreseeable future, a permanent wardship order may be made, with or without access. In some cases, the child will grow up in foster care, but may have regular contact with his or her family. In other cases, where adoption is a possibility, access to the biological family may be terminated so that the child may be placed in an adoptive home.

In most situations, child protection cases proceed on a "consent" basis. This means that the child protection agency has discussed the concerns it has with the parties and their lawyers (if they are represented), and they are in agreement as to the order that the court will be asked to make. In cases where a child is represented by a lawyer, that lawyer will be included in all discussions and part of any agreement. In a "consent" case, where the facts are generally agreed upon and the order is not opposed by any of the parties, the proceedings can be completed within a few minutes on the basis of statements by the lawyers, signed consents, "Agreed Statement of Facts" or "Minutes of Settlement," usually without the necessity of witnesses. Often reports or affidavits (sworn written statements) that have been prepared by professionals concerning the child are filed with the consent of the parties. Sometimes, in consent cases, the worker from the child protection agency will offer brief evidence to summarize the factual basis for the order requested.

While many child protection cases are resolved on a "consent basis," in some cases the finding of abuse or neglect is being opposed by the parent or caregiver. In many instances, a judge will monitor or "case manage" these situations to ensure that children's lives are not unnecessarily in limbo. Often a judge will hold "conferences" in an attempt to explore the possibilities of settling the issues between the parties. Where this is not possible, the judge will be asked to set a date for a full contested trial. At the trial it will be necessary to call all evidence that will permit the court to make a determination of whether or not a child is in need of protective services.

As in criminal proceedings, adjournments are common in child protection matters. They may be requested to permit the parties to obtain legal aid and to retain counsel, for plans to be put together and investigated by the agency, for completion of assessments and so forth. When an adjournment is granted, an important issue for the judge to resolve is where the child will reside pending trial.

Professional witnesses are not usually asked to attend these adjournment dates. However, if there is a dispute about whether the child will remain in parental care pending trial, it may be necessary to have professional testimony to assist the judge in determining the level of risk for a child remaining with a parent or relative. Most often at this interim stage, such professional evidence is received by a report or affidavit so that the professional's attendance in court is not necessary.

There are two main issues to be decided at a trial in a child protection case. The first is *whether or not the child has been, or there is a risk that a child is likely to be, abused or neglected.* If the child is found to have been abused or neglected or is at risk of abuse or neglect, then the court must decide the second issue, namely, what order is *appropriate to protect that child in the future.* Professionals who have worked with the child may be called to testify about either or both of these issues: whether the child has been abused or neglected or is otherwise "in need of protection" and, if so, what type of order would be most appropriate. At least in theory, the issue of the need for protection is distinct from the question of what type of order should be made. In some cases, therefore, the judge divides a contested hearing into two distinct phases, which might require a witness to give testimony twice in one proceeding, albeit about two different but related issues. In many cases, the two issues are dealt with in a single hearing.

There is also a process for judicial review of temporary wardship and supervision orders. When a court is reviewing a previously made order, the court may be concerned only with the second issue, that of making an appropriate order for the child's protection.

The issues in a child protection case can vary greatly. If you are called upon to give evidence in a case involving abuse or neglect, there are a number of issues that the court might consider relevant.

On the issue of whether abuse or neglect occurred or is likely to occur:

- observations of physical evidence of possible abuse or neglect, and statements made by the child about the origin of the injuries (e.g., a teacher testifying about a bruise observed on a pupil and the child's explanation);
- medical findings of abuse, neglect or a medical or developmental condition that requires attention;
- marital relationship difficulties that would render a child at risk physically or emotionally (e.g., violence, frequent separations and arguments);
- evidence of a medical or psychiatric condition or substance addiction by a parent that renders the child at risk (e.g., observations by a public health nurse that a parent is intoxicated while caring for a young child);
- statements made by the parties (usually the parents or the child) that would indicate a need for protection (e.g., a recreation worker testifying about parental threats of severe punishment);
- evidence of severe emotional stress in a child that the caregiver is not addressing (e.g., child is crying incessantly, wetting, clinging to teacher);
- evidence of any of the above in relation to a sibling or another child in the care of the parent or caregiver that might give rise to a substantial risk finding for abuse or neglect of a child while in that person's care;

- lack of co-operation and/or follow-through in the basic care of a child by the caregiver (e.g., nurse visited frequently and pointed out hazards to be eliminated and the parents failed to take necessary steps);
- effects of abuse or neglect on the child;
- the impact on children of observing domestic violence;
- where an application is being made to introduce statements by the child to a witness, evidence of the trauma that testifying would cause the child, and the reliability of statements made by the child (referred to as a *Khan* application).

On the issue of the appropriate type of intervention (disposition):

- whether the child can remain safely at home and, if so, under what conditions, or, alternatively, whether removal is necessary;
- what contact, if any, is in the child's best interests if removal from a parent is necessary;
- what services should be offered to the family to deal with the identified protection problem(s).

Child Abuse Protocols

Most jurisdictions have developed protocols for the joint investigations of allegations of sexual abuse by child protection and police personnel. These protocols help to define the roles and relationships between police and child protection services, and allow for a more co-ordinated response from both systems. In many cases, the protocols specifically call for a teamwork approach between child protection and criminal justice professionals. In most cases, the protocols are available upon request.

Custody and Access Disputes

Following separation or divorce, parents may bring an application to court concerning custody or access. Individuals who are not biological parents may also seek custody or access, but they are likely to obtain custody or access only if they have established a close relationship. A grandparent who has cared for a child may, for example, seek custody.

The majority of custody and access cases ultimately proceed on a "consent" basis. Often parents can agree on an arrangement for the care of their children and can also agree as to what constitutes a reasonable plan of access for the parent who is not living with the children. Sometimes parents will be encouraged to try mediation as a way of assisting them to resolve the issues of their separation. Increasingly parents consider some form of "joint custody," though this may not be appropriate where there are allegations of abuse or domestic violence or where communication between the parents is so strained that joint decisions are not possible. The notion of "joint custody" does not necessarily mean that time with the children is equally divided between the parents. In some cases, a joint custody parenting plan may look very much like a traditional custody/access plan. In other cases, it may not.

Mediation

Mediation is a form of alternate dispute resolution (ADR), meaning an alternative to litigation. Mediators are neutral professionals who attempt to facilitate discussions between parents so that they can resolve their disagreements. Mediators may have training as lawyers, psychologists or social workers. Mediation may deal with one issue, such an access dispute, or may be comprehensive and deal with all issues. Mediation is usually voluntary, although in civil disputes other than family cases, it may be mandatory.

In "closed" mediation, which is most common, all discussions are considered "without prejudice." This means that if the mediation does *not* result in an agreement, nothing said during the mediation can be used in a subsequent court process. The outcome of mediation, when successful, may be used in a separation agreement or court order on consent of the parties or may result in the formulation of a "parenting plan."

Mediation is not appropriate in all cases. Where there is a concern that there is a power imbalance between the parties (for example, in cases of domestic violence) or where there is no room for discussion, mediation may not be an option.

Where parents disagree about custody or access, there will need to be a trial to determine what arrangements will be in the child's "best interests." If one parent alleges that the other has abused or neglected the child, a court may also be called upon to hear and rule upon evidence relating to the alleged abuse or neglect as an aspect of determining what is in the child's best interests.

In these proceedings, the court is obliged to make an order that is in the best interests of the child or children. Even where child protection issues exist, the court will still have to consider whether contact between the child and adult should occur in future.

In this type of proceeding you may be asked to provide evidence of

- your observations and opinions concerning the parenting ability of one or both parents;
- the relationship between the parent(s) and the child(ren);
- the needs of the child(ren);
- the level of conflict evident in the relationship between the parents (as relevant to the feasibility of joint custody, or unsupervised access);
- evidence of spousal abuse;
- indicators that a child is likely to have been abused or neglected;
- evidence of a child's fear of a parent;
- evidence that a parent may be attempting to influence the child against the other parent;
- reliability of a parent to produce the child for access visits;
- statements made by a child as to wishes regarding custody or visiting;
- statements made by a child concerning abuse or neglect;
- your opinion as to which parent is better able to meet the child's needs on a day-to-day basis.

Disclosure and Discovery

An aspect of having fair procedural rules is that parties to litigation are entitled to "know the case they will have to meet." This can take the form of "disclosure" of documents (requiring a party to provide copies of all relevant documents to the other party), as well as "discovery," the opportunity to question the opposing party and, in some situations, a witness, before trial.

The process of disclosure and discovery enables parties to prepare for a fair trial. Often, when a party learns of the strength of the other side's case, there will be a settlement of a civil case. In a criminal proceeding, the process of Crown disclosure often results in a plea bargain or guilty plea.

In criminal cases, only the Crown is obliged to provide pre-trial disclosure of documents. As discussed earlier (p.20), in indictable criminal proceedings the accused may have an opportunity to cross-examine witnesses in a preliminary inquiry.

In civil cases, there is usually an obligation on both parties to provide full disclosure of all documents in their possession relevant to the case before trial. The rules of court generally also permit some form of pre-trial discovery. Discoveries are held before a "special examiner." Discoveries are conducted in an office, not in a court room. The special examiner is not a judge, but is authorized to administer an oath or affirmation and ensures that a record is kept of the discovery. At a discovery, each lawyer will have the opportunity to ask questions of the other party. Occasionally one lawyer may instruct a client being asked questions not to answer a question; if there is a serious dispute about the propriety of a question, the lawyers may appear before a judge who will decide whether the question should be answered. A transcript of the discovery will often be prepared and may be used later at the trial, either submitted in evidence or as the basis for further cross-examination.

Professionals who are involved as witnesses in court proceedings are often asked to prepare reports that will be disclosed prior to trial to all parties in the litigation. Generally only parties to civil litigation are subject to pre-trial discovery examinations. However, in complex cases, a court order may be obtained to

44444

4444

444444

444444444

allow pre-trial examination of a witness. A person who is examined at a discovery should ask for a copy of the transcript before testifying in court, to allow for refreshing of memory.

THE LEGAL ACTORS

The Role of the Judge

Our legal system is developed from the English "adversary" system of justice. This system works on the assumption that if each party has an opportunity to present the evidence and arguments that support its position, a just decision will be the result. In the adversary system, the role of the judge has traditionally been that of a "dispassionate referee," one who makes rulings as called upon, but leaves it to the parties to decide what evidence to call and what questions to ask.

In practice, the role varies according to the personality and style of the individual judge and the nature of the proceedings. Some judges remain relatively passive in the proceedings, only ruling on issues raised by the parties themselves. Other judges take a more active role by questioning witnesses or commenting without prompting upon a lawyer's conduct of the case. In civil cases where the future welfare of a child is at stake, such as child protection or custody and access disputes, the judge may feel a special burden to ensure that the right decision is made and may take a more active role in questioning witnesses. Increasingly, especially in family law cases, individuals are appearing before the courts without legal representation; in these cases judges are also likely to be more involved in trying to ensure that the proceedings are fair.

Generally, the judge can be expected to:

- control the trial and ensure it remains within the rules of the law and procedure, and
- decide on the admissibility of evidence.

In a civil case or a criminal case without a jury, the judge will:

- make findings regarding the credibility of witnesses, and
- render judgement based upon the evidence presented.

In criminal matters, the judge will:

- ensure that the accused is afforded the protections of the law (e.g., right to counsel),
- rule as to whether or not the accused is guilty as charged, and
- pass sentence if the accused is convicted.

If there is a jury in a criminal case, the judge will:

- ensure that only legally admissible evidence goes before the jury,
- instruct the jury as to the law, and
- pass sentence if the accused is convicted.

If there is a jury in a criminal case, it is the responsibility of the jury to determine whether or not the facts support the charge and the accused is guilty.

The Role of the Crown Attorney in a Criminal Case

As the agent of the Attorney General (or Minister of Justice) of the Province, who is the chief law-enforcement officer for the province, the Crown Attorney is responsible for protecting society without infringing the rights of one of its members, the accused. The Crown Attorney is sometimes referred to as the "Crown Prosecutor" or simply as the "Crown."

The functions of the Crown Attorney are:

- to advise the police and screen cases for prosecution;
- to provide disclosure of relevant evidence to defense counsel, whether favourable or unfavourable to the Crown's case;
- to determine the necessary witnesses in the proceedings, and to prepare the witnesses for testifying;
- to examine Crown witnesses in chief and to cross-examine defense witnesses;
- to summarize the case for the judge (and jury, if applicable) and make submissions as to the appropriate verdict at the conclusion of the evidence;

- to offer submissions as to the appropriate sentence if there is a conviction when called upon to do so by the judge.

It should be recognized that, when engaged as a prosecutor, the lawyer's prime duty is not to seek to convict but to see that justice is done through a fair trial. The prosecutor exercises a public function involving much discretion and power and must act fairly and dispassionately. Those who work with victims should recognize that the Crown Attorney does not take instructions from the alleged victim (or "complainant") or "represent" that person's interests in court.

The Role of Defence Counsel in a Criminal Case

As representative of the accused in a criminal matter, the defence lawyer can be expected to:

- ensure a fair trial for the accused;
- attempt to raise a reasonable doubt as to the guilt of the accused by calling witnesses, cross-examining the Crown's witnesses, or arguing about the admissibility or weight that should be attached to the evidence presented by the Crown. The accused is not, however, obliged to call evidence or testify in a criminal case;
- to make submissions on sentence, if there is a conviction.

The Role of Counsel for a Child Protection Agency

The functions of the lawyer who represents a child protection agency are:

- to advise social workers regarding child protection matters;
- to provide disclosure to parents' counsel and counsel for the child;
- to determine the necessary witnesses in the proceedings and to prepare the witnesses for testifying;
- to present relevant evidence relating to child protection cases so that the court may make an informed decision regarding the case;

- to offer submissions as to whether a child is in need of protective services and, if so, the order that is necessary to protect the child.

The Role of the Parent's Lawyer in a Child Protection Case

As representative of a parent or caregiver in a child protection matter, the parent's lawyer can be expected to protect parental rights by:

- challenging the grounds for the intervention;
- demonstrating that the plan of the agency is defective;
- establishing that an order is not necessary, or that a less intrusive order is adequate to protect the child;
- presenting an alternative plan by the parent or extended family members.

The Role of the Child's Lawyer in a Child Protection Case

In a number of provinces, a lawyer may be appointed to represent a child in a protection case or a custody or access dispute between parents. A lawyer for the child will:

- put forward the position expressed by the child, if the child is old enough to instruct the lawyer and the child wishes to do so;
- call witnesses or cross-examine to ensure all relevant evidence is heard by the judge.

FUNDAMENTAL FAIRNESS

The justice system is very concerned about notions of fairness. Many of the rules that have developed surrounding the requirements of "notice" (being advised of the time, place and issues of a hearing and avoiding last minute "surprises") and admissibility of evidence (rules about what a judge can properly consider as evidence) have as their basis the objective of creating a process that is fair to all the affected parties.

The criminal process is concerned primarily with balancing *fairness to the accused* and *protection of the public*. Many of the rights of the accused are now embodied in and extended by the *Canadian Charter of Rights and Freedoms*.

In Canada, the legal process has also become somewhat more sensitive in the past few years to the rights of victims as well as those of accused persons. The use of Victim Impact Statements (statements submitted to the sentencing judge about the effects of the crime on the victim) is an example of greater sensitivity to the victims of crime in the criminal process. However, the right of an accused person to a fair trial usually takes precedence over the rights of an apparent victim, even if the victim is a child.

In civil proceedings involving two private citizens, such as two parents seeking custody, the court will strive to balance the rights of the two parties. However, in a civil proceeding where a child protection agency of the state is arrayed against a private citizen, there will be an onus on the state to prove its case. Parents in a child protection case are threatened with the loss of custody of their child as a result of the action of an agency of the state and are normally entitled to be treated in accordance with the principles of fundamental fairness. Judges in a protection case will ensure that basic legal and procedural rights are respected, even if this results in a more adversarial or lengthy proceeding than might be desirable from the perspective of some of the professionals involved.

In a criminal case, examples of the principles of fundamental fairness at work in the courtroom include:

- the right of the accused to remain silent;
- the right of the accused to know the case against him or her;
- the right to be presumed innocent until proven guilty;
- the right to make full answer and defense.

In all cases, the principles of fundamental justice include:

- the right of an affected party to be notified of court proceedings;
- the right to attend the proceedings;

- the right to be represented by a lawyer;
- the right of a party or witness to a translator, if necessary;
- the right to be served notice of any documents to be filed in court by the other side, and to be provided copies on request;
- the right to cross-examine any witness called by the other side;
- the right to present the "other side of the story";
- the right to have a case decided by a judge or decision-maker about whom there is not reasonable concern of bias.

HIGHLIGHTS OF CHAPTER 1

This chapter considered some of the basic principles that guide our court system, the roles of the various players in the courtroom and the main types of proceedings a professional may be involved in as a witness on behalf of a child. What follows are some important points to remember.

The sources of law are:

- the Constitution, which divides responsibility for law-making between the federal and provincial governments, and contains the *Canadian Charter of Rights and Freedoms,* which guarantees certain rights for the individual involved with the government or its agencies;
- statute law, which is enacted by the federal or provincial governments;
- legal precedents that assist or sometimes bind a court dealing with the same issue as an earlier judgement;
- international law, such as the *United Nations Convention on the Rights of the Child,* which may also influence how courts deal with cases affecting children.

The kinds of proceedings are:

- *criminal proceedings,* where the Crown must prove its case "beyond a reasonable doubt";
- *civil proceedings,* where the party seeking an order must prove its case "on the balance of probabilities."

All proceedings, whether criminal or civil are governed by the principles of *fundamental fairness.*

CHAPTER 2

LEARNING HOW LAWYERS THINK AND ACT

L ike other professionals, lawyers are bound by a code of ethics that guides them in their day-to-day interactions. However, the orientation and ethical constraints of lawyers are often very different from those of other professionals. For some witnesses, questioning by a lawyer is particularly intimidating because the professional orientation of a lawyer is so removed from those of other "helping" professions. In this chapter we provide some questions and answers that we hope will help you to understand lawyers better.

HOW CAN A LAWYER REPRESENT A PERSON WHO HAS ALLEGEDLY ABUSED A CHILD?

It must be appreciated that not everyone who is charged with an offence is in fact guilty. The police do make errors in investigating cases. Further, on occasion the police may be influenced by bias or sympathy for an alleged victim to lay charges against someone who may not be guilty. Indeed, despite the legal presumption of innocence, there have been a few documented cases in Canada of individuals being wrongfully convicted and serving lengthy jail sentences before their innocence has been established by forensic evidence. However, most of those who are charged with offences are in fact guilty; most accused persons ultimately plead guilty.

Lawyers have professional responsibilities to their clients that may at times seem difficult for the layperson to understand. It is important to keep in mind that the lawyer who is acting for an "unpopular" party in a proceeding often does not personally share the values or views of the client. It is a basic tenet of the legal profession that every person is entitled to representation, particularly when there are criminal charges, no matter how unpopular the client or how heinous the allegations. The ethical code that governs lawyers provides that

> when acting as an advocate, a lawyer shall represent the client resolutely and honourably within the limits of the law while treating the tribunal with candour, fairness, courtesy, and respect.[7]

While the duty to act as advocate is tempered by the duty to discourage purely malicious proceedings, it is clear that the duty of a lawyer as an advocate is a high one. In the case of criminal prosecutions, the duty of a defence lawyer goes even further than the general duty to advocate.

> When defending an accused person the lawyer's duty is to protect the client as far as possible from being convicted except by a tribunal of competent jurisdiction and upon legal evidence sufficient to support a conviction for the offence with which the client is charged. Accordingly, and notwithstanding the lawyer's private opinion on credibility or the merits, a lawyer may properly rely upon any evidence or defences including so-called technicalities not known to be false or fraudulent.[8]

HOW CAN A LAWYER HELP AN ACCUSED WHO APPEARS GUILTY TO DENY HIS GUILT?

Lawyers cannot introduce evidence that they *know* to be false. If an accused client confesses guilt to his lawyer, the lawyer cannot call the client as a witness to lie about the alleged crime.

---

[7]   Law Society of Upper Canada, *Rules of Professional Conduct* (2000), Rule 4.01(1).

[8]   Ibid.

However, even if the client has confessed to his lawyer, it is not only perfectly acceptable but it is the duty of the defence lawyer to vigorously test the Crown's case. In the case of a criminal prosecution, where the onus is on the Crown to prove its case beyond a reasonable doubt, it may on occasion be the sole role of counsel for the accused to focus on the deficiencies of the Crown's case, without ever calling evidence and without asserting that the accused did not actually commit the crime.

In practice, if the client confesses guilt to his lawyer, the prosecution will usually have significant evidence of guilt as well, and the lawyer will advise the accused of the advantages of pleading guilty and showing remorse in terms of more lenient sentencing by the court. Ultimately, however, the client must decide whether to plead guilty or to have a trial.

It is rare for the client to confess guilt to his lawyer and insist on a trial. More commonly, for a variety of psychological and tactical reasons, those who are in fact guilty but want a trial will usually try to deceive both their lawyer and the court. The lawyer may personally believe that the client is guilty, but if the client maintains his innocence, the lawyer must assist the client in telling his story to the court. Of course, if the Crown's case is strong or the story of the accused seems implausible, the lawyer has a professional duty to inform the client of this and to discuss the likely outcome of a trial.

It should also be appreciated that the fact that an accused in a criminal case does not testify does not mean that the accused is guilty. In some cases an accused person may in fact be innocent but may decide not to testify for tactical reasons. This may occur if the accused has a lengthy criminal record, which generally can only be revealed at trial if he testifies. The accused may be concerned that by taking the witness stand, his or her criminal record may become known to the court and result in an improper inference of guilt for the charge before the court. As a matter of law, the *Charter of Rights* guarantees the right to silence, and it is wrong for a judge or lawyer to suggest that a jury should infer guilt from the silence of the accused. However, in practice, the failure of an accused to testify may affect how some jurors assess a case.

In a civil case, there is no "right to silence." The failure to testify or deny an allegation can properly be the basis of an inference that the person accepts the truth of the allegation.

WHY IS THE DEFENCE COUNSEL SO AGGRESSIVE COMPARED TO THE CROWN OR AGENCY LAWYER?

In describing the role of the lawyer, it is important to distinguish between the role of a lawyer who is acting for a private client, such as the accused in a criminal case or a parent in a child protection or custody proceeding, from that of a lawyer representing the Crown or the child protection agency in a child welfare matter.

The lawyer who represents "the Crown" has some special duties not ascribed to the pure advocate acting on behalf of a citizen. The representative of the Crown has a duty to see that "justice is done" through a fair trial. The duty to act fairly emerges from the role of prosecutor as a public servant with a great deal of discretion and power. For example, the prosecutor "should make timely disclosure to defence counsel or directly to an unrepresented accused of all relevant and known facts and witnesses, whether tending to show guilt or innocence."[9] The lawyer representing a child protection agency has a similar ethical obligation.[10]

As explained by the Supreme Court of Canada,

> it cannot be overemphasized that the purpose of a criminal prosecution is not to obtain a conviction, it is to lay before a jury [or judge] what the Crown considers to be credible evidence relevant to what is alleged to be a crime.... The role of the prosecutor excludes any notion of winning or losing; his function is a matter of public duty than which in public life

[9] Law Society of Upper Canada, *Rules of Professional Conduct* (2000), Commentary to Rule 4.01(3).

[10] See *Children's Aid Society of Durham* v. *K.W.* (1990), 72 O.R.(2d) 711 (Prov. Ct.), where Judge Webster expressed doubts about the position of a child protection agency that had argued that it was not obliged to present the testimony of a police officer "that ... was not of benefit to their case." Some parts of the final decision in this case were reversed on appeal, but there was no adverse comment on this point (1992), 5 O.F.L.R. 084 (C.A.).

there can be none charged with greater personal responsibility.[11]

Prosecutors play a dual role as both administrators of justice
and as advocates. While as advocates they have a responsibility
to present the prosecution's case in "forcible and direct
language," they must avoid being inflammatory or unfair.[12] As
administrators of justice, Crown prosecutors have a responsibility
to see that the innocent are not prosecuted or convicted and a
duty to discontinue a prosecution if there is not a reasonable likelihood that a conviction will be obtained.

DO LAWYERS HAVE ANY RESPONSIBILITY TO THE COURT?

The lawyer has a duty to the court to uphold the integrity of the
legal process. A lawyer cannot knowingly mislead the court. As
one can imagine, a lawyer sometimes has difficulty balancing
duty to the client with duty to the court when they are in conflict.

DO LAWYERS FOR PARENTS HAVE ANY RESPONSIBILITIES TO CHILDREN?

It is now accepted among lawyers that special ethical duties
may arise in civil proceedings that will likely affect the health,
welfare or security of a child. The *Rules of Professional Conduct* that
govern Ontario lawyers now require that, in such proceedings, "a
lawyer should advise the client to take into account the best interests of the child, where this can be done without prejudicing the
legitimate interests of the client."[13]

---

[11] *Boucher* v. *R.*, [1955] S.C.R. 16, at 23-24, by Rand J.

[12] Gavin Mackenzie, *Lawyers and Ethics: Professional Responsibility and Discipline* (Toronto: Carswell, 1993), 64.

[13] Law Society of Upper Canada, *Rules of Professional Conduct* (2000), Rule 4.01(1). Commentary.

WHO MAKES THE DECISIONS ABOUT HOW A CASE PROCEEDS, THE LAWYER OR THE CLIENT?

While the lawyer has responsibility for providing advice to the client, it is ultimately the client who must make the major decisions about how a case will be handled. Although some decisions about procedural or evidentiary matters are to be made by the lawyer, a lawyer has a duty to take instructions from a client about the most important aspects of the case. In a criminal proceeding, it is the client who must decide whether or not to plead guilty, and whether or not to testify. In a civil case, such as one involving custody or access, it is the client who must decide whether to litigate or settle. Therefore, despite the most vigorous attempts to advise the client to settle a case, a lawyer may find him or herself in a contested proceeding.

MUST A LAWYER KEEP A CLIENT'S SECRETS?

One of the fundamental duties of a lawyer is the duty of confidentiality. Unless the release of information is authorized by the client, a lawyer must keep all information received from the client in strict confidence. Indeed, the fact that a person has consulted with a lawyer may be confidential. Also, a lawyer must not share information gained from one client with another client.

The rule of "solicitor-client" privilege, which prohibits a lawyer from disclosing information received from a client, is intended to assure clients that they can fully share information about their situation with their lawyer and thus receive the fullest advice. If a client confesses to his lawyer that he is guilty of a crime, the lawyer cannot report this to the police or otherwise disclose this without the client's consent.

While a lawyer must keep a client's confidences, the lawyer also has a duty not to obstruct the administration of justice. As noted above, if the client confesses guilt, the lawyer cannot assist the client in actually lying to the court about the crime, although the client is not obliged to admit his guilt in court and the lawyer may still argue that the Crown has not proven its case beyond a reasonable doubt. If a client delivers physical evidence of a crime to the lawyer, such as the gun used in a crime, the lawyer has an obligation to ensure that this evidence comes into the hands of the police, although this should be done in a way that does not directly implicate the client. The lawyer could have another lawyer deliver the evidence to the police.

Just as a lawyer must keep confidential information received from the client, information received by the lawyer must, generally speaking, be shared with the client. It is normally not possible, unless the client agrees, for a therapist or other professional to provide a report to a lawyer that is not also to be shared with the client.

DO LAWYERS HAVE A DUTY TO REPORT CHILD ABUSE?

In Ontario, as in most provinces, child abuse reporting legislation specifically states that it does *not* override solicitor-client privilege. However, there may be circumstances in which there is sufficiently grave risk to the welfare of a child or other vulnerable person that a lawyer will be justified in sharing information learned from a client with child welfare authorities or the police. The *Ontario Rules of Professional Conduct* provide that

> where a lawyer believes upon reasonable grounds that there is an imminent risk to an identifiable person or group of death or serious bodily harm, including serious psychological harm that substantially interferes with health or well-being, the lawyer *may* disclose ... confidential information where it is necessary to do so in order to prevent the death or harm, but shall not disclose more information than is required.[14]

This rule might justify the disclosure to a child protection agency by a lawyer for a child that the client has threatened to commit suicide or has disclosed allegations of incest. Even in this situation, however, the lawyer is likely to encourage the child to directly disclose the abuse to a social worker or other trusted adult.

---

[14] Law Society of Upper Canada (2000), Rule 2.03(3). Emphasis added.

This rule applies only to situations where there is a threat to future well-being and does not justify disclosure of past crimes if there is no reasonable prospect of recurrence. If the authorities are aware of the risk to a child, this rule does not justify further disclosure. Therefore, if the child protection agency has received a report of child abuse and a parent has been charged, this rule would not justify a lawyer for the parent disclosing further information to confirm the agency's belief that abuse occurred. Further, this rule only *permits* rather than *requiring* disclosure, and lawyers are sometimes left struggling with difficult ethical issues without clear guidance.

WILL THE LAWYER WHO CALLS ME AS A WITNESS ACT AS MY LAWYER?

The lawyer who calls a person as a witness will often meet with the witness before court to prepare the witness for court. That lawyer will be the first to ask the witness questions on what is called "examination-in-chief." After examination-in-chief, there will be cross-examination by counsel for the opposing party.

Sometimes the lawyer who has called a witness will object to questions during cross-examination to prevent harassment or unfair questioning, but this lawyer is not representing the witness. In particular, if a witness is called to testify by a Crown Attorney or the lawyer for a child protection agency, these lawyers have a duty to ensure that justice is done, and not to interfere with a probing, but appropriate cross-examination. The cross-examining counsel has a large degree of discretion as to the scope and subject matter of questioning. Questions that seem repetitive or rude may be legally proper. Most judges lean over backwards to give parent's counsel (in a child protection case) or counsel for the accused (in a criminal case) an opportunity to explore the issues of the case as they see them. Because of the intrusive nature of these proceedings, the professional who testifies in these cases has to expect a degree of tolerance from the judge for a style of questioning that might not be appropriate in another context, such as a job interview or a case conference.

As a rule, the professional witness is expected to attempt to answer any relevant question provided he or she knows the answer, no matter how difficult. When the questions become repetitive, or the manner of questioning is particularly hostile, it is not uncommon for the Crown or agency lawyer to ask for the judge to intervene if the judge has not already done so. In most cases, professional witnesses are appreciated by all parties as sharing their objective observations in a difficult decision-making process, and while the questions put to them may be challenging, counsel rarely gain an advantage for a client by being rude to a witness.

WHAT CAN I EXPECT FROM THE LAWYER WHO REPRESENTS A CHILD IN THE PROCEEDINGS?

In some provinces, including Ontario, it is not uncommon to have lawyers acting on behalf of children in child protection or custody cases involving allegations of abuse or neglect. Sometimes the child in a protection case is old enough to have views that the judge will want to consider when making his or her decision. Likewise, in a custody or access dispute, the lawyer for a child can help to make the child's needs and wishes heard by the judge and by the parents. Not infrequently, a child's lawyer plays a vital role in encouraging the settlement of disputes between parents, or disputes between a child protection agency and a family.

The role of lawyers representing children varies depending upon the age of the child, the capacity of the child, the type of proceedings and the style of the lawyer. It is impossible for a lawyer to know what a very young child wishes as the outcome for the proceeding, and the lawyer must often rely on his or her own best judgement of what is in the best interests of the child. As a child matures and becomes capable of instructing a lawyer as to his or her wishes, the role moves towards that of the advocate for the child, just as for an adult client. There are understandably many grey areas, and different lawyers have their own views about the role of child's counsel. In some cases it may be difficult to know what approach is being taken by the child's lawyer. It may be a good idea to avoid making assumptions and to ask directly what position is being taken on behalf of the child.

WHY DO LAWYERS ON THE OPPOSITE SIDE OF A CASE REFER TO EACH OTHER AS "MY FRIEND"?

This term, "my friend" as a reference to opposing counsel, is borrowed from English court traditions, where an atmosphere of courtesy in the courtroom was encouraged. The use of this term suggests that counsel have respect for each other, even though the parties may be hostile towards one another. Some lawyers use the phrase "my friend" or "my learned friend" in referring to counsel for the other side. While the use of such expressions may be disconcerting to lay persons, it does not mean that the client will be any less energetically represented.

WHY DO LAWYERS SPEND SO MUCH TIME ARGUING IN COURT?

Although non-lawyers tend to think of the law as clear and straightforward, it is, in fact, full of ambiguity and contradictions. Often the legal rule that governs a situation is clear, but there is uncertainty about the facts of the case or how they apply to the rule. Lawyers are trained to identify uncertainty and ambiguities, to make various arguments that support the position of their client and to urge the judge to accept the approach that is favourable to their client.

DO ALL CASES PROCEED TO THE TRIAL STAGE?

The vast majority of cases settle at some point before a full-blown trial. Recognizing the high emotional and financial cost of contested court hearings, there are a number of procedures intended to encourage settlement of cases. This begins by making sure that the parties share all relevant information with each other, long before the courtroom door. Most provinces have incorporated a "pre-trial conference" or "settlement conference" requirement or option, which is an informal discussion before a judge. The judge listens to the positions and arguments of the parties and offers suggestions for the resolution of the case. This judge would not normally be the judge hearing the case if it were to go to trial.

If the parties in a civil proceeding agree to settle the case, the judge will almost always accept this. In theory, however, in cases relating to children, a judge may have some responsibility to protect the interests of a child. In practice, the civil cases in which judges most commonly intervene to reject a settlement involve child support, where judges can easily determine by reference to *Child Support Guidelines* whether adequate provision has been made for the child. Even in these cases, most judges accept a settlement reached by the parties.

As a possible witness at a trial, you may be called upon to provide a written report or affidavit at the pre-trial stage outlining the kind of evidence you would be giving if the matter proceeded to a trial. Not infrequently, the provision of a report will facilitate a settlement or make it unnecessary for the professional to testify.

In a criminal case, there is an obligation on the Crown to fully disclose its case to the accused before trial, but the accused has no similar obligation. There are likely to be "resolution conferences" even in criminal cases that have as their objective the resolution of a case by means of a guilty plea with a joint submission as to sentence (called "plea bargaining" or "plea negotiations"). While the judge is not bound by an agreement as to sentence, judges usually accept joint submissions as the basis for a sentence. In some cases, counsel for the accused can meet with the Crown prosecutor before court and persuade the Crown that there is no reasonable prospect for a conviction and that the charges should be dropped, or that the case is appropriate for some form of diversion.

HIGHLIGHTS OF CHAPTER 2

This chapter looked at some of the ethical duties of lawyers, and how those duties may differ depending upon whether the lawyer is representing an individual, a child or a government agency.

The following points are important to remember:

- Lawyers are bound by a code of professional conduct.
- Lawyers are under a duty to advocate a client's position even when the lawyer may not personally agree with the client's views.
- Lawyers who represent the Crown in a criminal case or a child protection agency in a child protection case have special duties that include ensuring that the legal process is fair and that relevant evidence is disclosed prior to trial and is put before the court, whether or not it supports their case.
- Lawyers for children may act according to the child's wishes or best interests, depending upon the situation.

CHAPTER 3

CONFIDENTIALITY AND THE DISCLOSURE OF INFORMATION BY PROFESSIONALS

A lmost all professionals are concerned with issues of confidentiality and the potential difficulties created by the disclosure of information in the legal process.

Legislation imposes a duty of confidentiality upon many professionals, such as teachers and doctors. Other professionals, such as social workers in private practice, are required by their professional code of ethics to protect the information gained in the counselling process.

Many of the confidentiality issues raised in the context of proceedings involving abuse or neglect of children do not have clear answers. This chapter offers a discussion to assist you in understanding some of the issues. We suggest, however, that you consider obtaining legal advice if you are unsure about how much and when to share information in a particular situation. Failure to obey the legal rules about confidentiality and improper disclosure may have legal consequences for professionals and jeopardize their relationship with clients and patients. Improper disclosure of information may also cause embarrassment, trauma or a loss of trust for parents and children.

THE DUTY TO REPORT SUSPECTED CHILD ABUSE OR NEGLECT

While almost all professionals are under either ethical or legal constraints to keep information confidential, legislation in all provinces makes clear that there is a duty to report suspected child abuse or neglect. The need to protect children from the risk of harm justifies overriding obligations of confidentiality.

Section 72 of the Ontario *Child and Family Services Act* establishes the duty of professionals to report child abuse and provides as follows:

> 72.(1) *Duty to report child in need of protection*–Despite the provisions of any other Act, if a person, including a person who performs professional or official duties with respect to children, has reasonable grounds to suspect one of the following, the person shall forthwith report the suspicion and the information upon which it is based to a [children's aid] society:
>
> 1. The child has suffered physical harm, inflicted by the person having charge of the child or caused or resulting from that person's,
>
>> i. failure to adequately care for, provide for, supervise or protect the child, or
>>
>> ii. pattern of neglect in caring for, providing for, supervising or protecting the child.
>
> 2. There is a risk that the child is likely to suffer physical harm inflicted by the person having charge of the child or caused by or resulting from that person's,
>
>> i. failure to adequately care for, provide for, supervise or protect the child, or
>>
>> ii. pattern of neglect in caring for, providing for, supervising or protecting the child.
>
> 3. The child has been sexually molested or sexually exploited, by the person having charge of the child or by another person where the person having charge of the child knows or should know of the possibility of sexual molestation or sexual exploitation and fails to protect the child.
>
> 4. There is a risk that the child is likely to be sexually molested or sexually exploited as described in paragraph 3.
>
> 5. The child requires medical treatment to cure, prevent or alleviate physical harm or suffering and the child's parent or the person having charge of the child does not provide or refuses or is unavailable or unable to consent to, the treatment.

6. The child has suffered emotional harm, demonstrated by serious,

   i. anxiety,

   ii. depression,

   iii. withdrawal,

   iv. self-destructive or aggressive behaviour, or

   v. delayed development,

   and there are reasonable grounds to believe that the emotional harm suffered by the child results from the actions, failure to act or pattern of neglect on the part of the child's parent or the person having charge of the child.

7. The child has suffered emotional harm of the kind described in subparagraph i, ii, iii, iv or v of paragraph 6 and the child's parent or the person having charge of the child does not provide, or refuses or is unavailable or unable to consent to, services or treatment to remedy or alleviate the harm.

8. There is a risk that the child is likely to suffer emotional harm of the kind described in subparagraph i, ii, iii, iv or v of paragraph 6 resulting from the actions, failure to act or pattern of neglect on the part of the child's parent or the person having charge of the child.

9. There is a risk that the child is likely to suffer emotional harm of the kind described in subparagraph i, ii, iii, iv or v of paragraph 6 and that the child's parent or the person having charge of the child does not provide, or refuses or is unavailable or unable to consent to, services or treatment to prevent the harm.

10. The child suffers from a mental, emotional or developmental condition that, if not remedied, could seriously impair the child's development and the child's parent or the person having charge of the child does not provide, or refuses or is unavailable or unable to consent to, treatment to remedy or alleviate the condition.

11. The child has been abandoned, the child's parent has died or is unavailable to exercise his or her custodial rights over the child and has not made adequate provision for the child's care and custody, or the child is in a residential placement and the parent refuses or is unable or unwilling to resume the child's care and custody.

12. The child is less than 12 years old and has on more than one occasion injured another person or caused serious damage to another person's property, services or treatment are necessary to prevent a recurrence and the child's parent or the person in charge of the child does not provide, or refuses or is unavailable or unable to consent to, those services or treatment.

13. The child is less than 12 years old and has on more than one occasion injured another person or caused loss or damage to another person's property, with the encouragement of the person having charge of the child or because of that person's failure or inability to supervise the child adequately.

(2) *Ongoing duty to report*–A person who has additional reasonable grounds to suspect one of the matters set out in subsection (1) shall make a further report under subsection (1) even if he or she has made previous reports with respect to the same child.

(3) *Person must report directly*–A person who has a duty to report a matter under subsection (1) or (2) shall make the report directly to the society and shall not rely on any other person to report on his or her behalf.

(4) *Offence*–A person referred to in subsection (5) is guilty of an offence if,

(a) he or she contravenes subsection (1) or (2) by not reporting a suspicion; and

(b) the information on which it was based was obtained in the course of his or her professional or official duties.

(5) *Same*–Subsection (4) applies to every person who performs professional or official duties with respect to children including,

(a) a health care professional, including a physician, nurse, dentist, pharmacist and psychologist;

(b) a teacher, school principal, social worker, family counsellor, priest, rabbi, member of the clergy, operator or employee of a day nursery and youth and recreation worker;

(c) a peace officer and a coroner;

(d) a solicitor; and

(e) a service provider and an employee of a service provider.

(6) *Same*–In clause (5)(b), "youth and recreation worker" does not include a volunteer.

(6.1) *Same*–A director, officer or employee of a corporation who authorizes, permits, or concurs in a contravention of an offence under subsection (4) by an employee of the corporation is guilty of an offence.

(6.2) *Same*–A person convicted of an offence under subsection (4) or (6.1) is liable to a fine of not more than $1000.

(7) *Section overrides privilege*–This section applies although the information reported may be confidential or privileged, and no action for making the report shall be instituted against a person who acts in accordance with this section unless the person acts maliciously or without reasonable grounds for the suspicion.

(8) *Exception: solicitor client privilege*–Nothing in this section abrogates any privilege that may exist between a solicitor and his or her client.

Notice that subsection 72(1) requires the reporting of not only *the suspicion of abuse or neglect itself,* but also *the information on which it is based.* Subsection 72(7) makes clear that the obligation to report overrides the confidentiality provisions of any other statute. In order to encourage reporting, this section also provides civil immunity from actions such as libel or slander for those who report in good faith in cases in which it turns out that the allegations are unfounded, as long as the report is made in good faith.

The only exception to the professional duty to report child abuse is found in subsection 72(8), which applies if the information results from communication between a lawyer and a client, the so-called "solicitor-client" privilege. As discussed in chapter 2, there may be situations in which there is high risk to a child. However, there has not yet been a report of abuse in which a lawyer may choose to decide to breach the solicitor-client privilege in order to protect a child, and a lawyer is never obliged to report based on disclosures from a client.

Subsection 72(4) of the legislation makes it an offence for the professional to fail to comply with the reporting duty contained in subsection 72(1), with a maximum penalty of a fine of $1000.

At least for reporting purposes, the listed professionals are not only protected from any consequences resulting from a possible breach of the duty of confidentiality but, on the contrary, could face prosecution for failing to report suspected child protection concerns.

The current Ontario legislation has broadened the reporting criteria from abuse to a wider range of protection situations as outlined in subsection 72(1) above. Professionals such as doctors or teachers may face disciplinary sanctions from licensing bodies for failing to report "reasonable suspicions" of abuse, neglect or other grounds for finding a child in need of protection. Further, if a child suffers additional abuse as a result of a failure to report, there could be a civil suit for damages against the professional who failed to report.

When a professional reports a suspicion of protection concerns to a child protection agency, there is usually an expectation that the professional will co-operate in the court process that may result, although this is not always the case. Reporting anonymously is not a practical option for a professional who wishes to document compliance with the duty to report.

RECORDS AND DOCUMENTS

When a professional is requested to release written information about clients or patients, other than in the situation of a report of abuse to a child protection agency, it is important to be aware of the confidentiality issues involved. Generally speaking, the release of information in any other circumstances should be offered only on a valid signed consent, or pursuant to a search warrant, subpoena, summons or court order.

Again, we emphasize the importance of familiarizing yourself with the policies in your profession or agency for the release of information and of obtaining a legal opinion where there is any question about your particular situation.

CONSENT TO DISCLOSE INFORMATION

Consents, to be valid in law, must be given by individuals who understand what they are doing and agree voluntarily (not as a result of coercion or duress) to provide the consent. The consent needs to be an informed one, which means the person needs to know exactly what information is intended to be shared, with whom and for what purpose. The safest practice is to obtain the consent to disclose information in writing, witnessed and dated, setting out the nature of the information to be shared, with whom it will be shared and for what purpose.

Sometimes there is some urgency to share information. If time does not permit the signing of consents, any oral consent to disclose information should be duly noted in the professional's file and followed up as soon as possible with a written consent.

Often, when court proceedings are anticipated, the lawyers representing the parties will agree that a certain professional has important information for a court hearing on the matter. Information about a child or family can be shared if the person or persons whose confidentiality rights would potentially be affected give permission through counsel to provide information to the other parties.

A consent is only legally valid if given by the person authorized to give it. Generally, a professional should obtain the consent of the patient or client from whom the information was obtained. One parent cannot normally give a valid consent to the release of information provided by the other, since the "confidentially right" to information about an adult rests with the person who provided the information. In some situations, a professional such as a family doctor may have obtained information from more than one person in a family; if the parents separate, the complexity of the situation or the records may make it very difficult to determine whose consent is required. In these cases, the record holder should obtain a consent from everyone who might have a "confidentiality" right, or insist upon a court order or summons before releasing information, or seek legal advise.

For younger children, the consent of a parent is usually sufficient for the release of information relating to the child. For a child who can understand the issues involved, however, it may be advisable to obtain the consent of the child as well as the parent before agreeing to release information to other parties. If the parents are separated, it would be desirable to have the consent of both parents for the release of information about the child. However, there is legal authority to support the view that either parent has the right to information about their child's health, education or welfare and can consent to the release of that information, unless one parent's rights in this regard have been limited by a separation agreement or court order.[15]

The parties should be encouraged to discuss issues about the release of documents with their lawyers if so represented, since a party may not fully realize the potential legal implications of signing a consent to the disclosure of information. A professional cannot force a party to seek legal advice, but you should encourage the party to discuss the consent with his or her lawyer before signing. If a party declines the opportunity to discuss the document with a lawyer, make a note about your discussions so that it is clear (if you are later questioned) that you did not attempt to interfere with the client's right to legal advice.

Sometimes the parties have retained a professional to assist them in resolving the issues before the court. For example, a psychiatrist might be retained to assess the family relationships and to make recommendations about the custody or access arrangements that would best meet a child's needs. If the professional is retained by one party, then the information in the hands of that profeessional belongs to that party until that party agrees to share it. If, however, the professional is retained jointly by the parties, it is usually understood that the information belongs to all the participants, and that the confidentiality issues, at least between the parties involved in the proceedings, have been waived.

---

[15] See, for example, Ontario *Children's Law Reform Act,* s. 20(5).

RELEASE OF INFORMATION IN RESPONSE TO SEARCH WARRANT OR COURT ORDER

If a case is the subject of investigation by the police or a child protection agency, other professionals may wish to co-operate. However, other than in situations involving the duty to report suspected child abuse or neglect, it is important to remember that the client's rights need to be respected, even where the "authorities" are involved, and information should not be improperly released. Where for any reason the necessary consents to the disclosure of information have not been obtained, records may be obtained by a party in the proceedings through a number of means.

The police may obtain a search warrant from a court to authorize the release of sensitive material if they can establish that there are reasonable grounds to believe that the material may contain evidence relating to the possible commission of a crime.

An accused person in a criminal case may also seek a court order for the production of records relating to a child who is the alleged victim of an offence.[16] The professional who has physical control of the records must receive notice of the request and may attend at court to contest the disclosure of the records to the accused. The record holder may have representation at the hearing to decide whether the records are to be disclosed. A judge will have to balance the interests of the accused to a fair trail against the privacy interests of the person to whom the records relate, and inspect the records before deciding whether they are to be disclosed.

Likewise, in Ontario, the Children's Aid Society is authorized under section 74 of the *Child and Family Services Act* to obtain a warrant or court order for the release of records where the records contain information that may be relevant to the consideration of whether a child is in need of protection. To obtain the order, however, the Children's Aid Society must establish that the custodian of the records has refused to release them. It may,

---

[16] *Criminal Code*, s. 278. 1 - 278. 9.

therefore, be necessary for you to provide the agency with a letter formally documenting your refusal to release the records in question. If you work in a hospital or other agency that is routinely asked by child protection agencies to share information, it may be advisable to establish a protocol for the management of requests for information so that mutual expectations are clarified. In some circumstances, especially with records relating to the mental health of a parent, it may be possible for the record holder to attend court and contest the disclosure of the records; the court will weigh any potential harm to the parent from disclosure against the risk to the child if the information is not disclosed.

Professionals who are served with a search warrant or court order to produce records and are concerned that disclosure may harm a client should obtain legal advice to ascertain whether the order can be challenged.

RESPONDING TO A SUBPOENA OR SUMMONS

If properly served, a subpoena in a criminal proceeding or a summons in a civil proceeding compels the witness to attend a proceeding on a given date. As well as requiring a person to attend court as a witness, a subpoena or summons will often require a witness to bring to court relevant records or written information in the witness's possession.

In a criminal case, the subpoena is obtained from the Justice of the Peace by the police, sometimes in consultation with the Crown Attorney. In civil matters, the summons is obtained from the Court administrator (who is a Justice of the Peace) by the party who requests the presence of the witness. It is the lawyer for that party who has the right to enforce the summons, or to release the witness from appearing.

If a witness fails to attend court without making proper arrangements with the lawyer who has arranged for the subpoena or summons, the consequences can be very serious. Providing that the witness has been served properly, and the anticipated evidence is important for the determination of the case, the witness might even face arrest for failing to appear.

Both a subpoena and a summons can request the witness to bring to court documentation in his or her possession. Technically, the witness is only compelled to release information, either written or verbal, from the witness stand and not before testifying. This means that prior to the hearing date, and even up to the point of waiting outside the courtroom door to be called as a witness, you are not obliged to release information to the parties.

If you are requested to bring documentation to court, it is wise to take a copy of the material and systematically to check the copy against your originals. That way, if a party requests that the documentation be made an exhibit, you can release your copy to the court and leave with your originals.

As a practical matter, many witnesses, once under summons or subpoena, will talk to the lawyer who has called them as a witness in advance of the trial itself. However, if a case is hotly contested, it may be advisable to avoid disclosing confidential information unless you are certain that this is legally permissible. You may wish to obtain independent legal advice or the consent of all parties as to when it is appropriate to release information.

Once on the witness stand, you are generally compelled to answer all "proper" questions to the best of your ability. The judge, if asked, will determine whether or not a question is proper. A question might be found to be improper where it is irrelevant (see "Relevance," page 74), or where the answer is privileged (see "Privilege," page 86).

HIGHLIGHTS OF CHAPTER 3

This chapter considered some of the difficult confidentiality issues facing a professional who is asked to testify. The following points are important to remember:

- Consult a lawyer if you are unsure of what information should be disclosed and to whom.

- The duty to report suspected child abuse (and in Ontario, other child protection concerns) in most provinces specifically overrides any obligation to keep information confidential.

- Other information should generally only be shared with the consent of the parties affected, or as a result of a search warrant, subpoena, summons or court order.

CHAPTER 4

TRIAL PROCEDURE

While it is impossible to describe all the kinds of court proceedings in detail, we will try to give you an idea of the most common aspects of the trial process so that you have an idea of what to expect in the courtroom.

We will focus on the procedure for a civil case. It is important to remember that your testimony is only one part of a larger context. Much of what we will be describing will take place before or after you testify.

INTRODUCTION OF THE PARTIES

The party initiating a civil proceeding is usually called the "applicant," or sometimes the "plaintiff" or "petitioner." The other party is usually known as the "respondent," but sometimes as the "defendant." In a child protection case the agency is usually the applicant, while in a custody or access dispute, the applicant is the person who first brought the case to the court system.

The applicant often begins the hearing by introducing all of the parties and their counsel to the presiding judge, noting names for the court record. Alternatively, the lawyers will identify themselves and their clients.

If the hearing is closed to the public (as for child protection proceedings) and there are any other persons in the courtroom, they may be asked to identify themselves to the court. Persons not directly involved in the case may be asked to leave the courtroom.

Where there are more than two parties, the order of questioning will be determined by the judge at the outset, as well as the order of evidence presented by the respondents.

CLARIFICATION OF POSITIONS

In a civil case, the parties are required to prepare documents setting out their case. For example, in Ontario the "applicant" (e.g., a children's aid society) will have commenced the proceedings by filing an "application," and the other parties (parents) will have filed an "answer." Other documents may also have been filed as well. These documents may be collectively referred to as "the pleadings" or "the record." The judge will have reviewed these documents before the trial commences.

Because the circumstances or positions of the parties may change during the period before a hearing, it is important for the lawyers to offer the judge up-to-date information regarding their position. If the issues in dispute have been narrowed as a result of informal discussion between the lawyers or as a result of a pre-trial conference, the judge will be told of what has been agreed to by the parties, and what remains contested. It is at this initial point that an "agreed statement of facts" would be offered to the court. If any documentary evidence is to go before the court with the consent of all parties, it is at this time that such evidence will usually be filed.

If the lawyers wish to make "opening statements" or a summary of the evidence and argument they will be presenting, such a statement might be offered at this time, or at the beginning of the presentation of the evidence in support of their client's case.

APPLICANT'S CASE

The applicant is required to put its evidence before the court first. The procedure ensures fairness to the respondent (the party who must respond) in knowing what evidence needs to be answered. The lawyer for the applicant calls each of his or her witnesses in turn and usually has discretion as to the order in which witnesses will be called to testify.

Before testifying, each witness will be asked to swear an oath or affirm (see "Oral Testimony," page 76). First the lawyer who has called the witness to give evidence will conduct an "examination-in-chief." Following this, the witness will be cross-examined by counsel for the other party or parties. The witness will then be re-examined if some issues raised in cross-examination require some further clarification. We will describe the process of examination and cross-examination in further detail in the following chapter ("Testifying in Court," page 93). Broadly speaking, in cross-examination there is considerably wider scope for questioning than in an examination-in-chief.

During the course of a witness testifying, the lawyer who is not doing the questioning may object to a particular question or line of questioning. The lawyers may argue about the appropriateness of the question or the admissibility of the answer, and the judge will rule on whether the question should be asked. The judge may instruct the witness to restrict the answer in some way (see "Testifying in Court," page 93).

The lawyer for either party has the discretion to determine the order in which his or her witnesses will testify. Usually the lawyer will attempt to follow a chronological or logical sequence, though sometimes a witness will testify "out of order" to facilitate the scheduling of the court appearance of a busy professional.

THE RESPONDENT'S CASE

Once the evidence for the applicant has been completed, the respondent will be given an opportunity to call witnesses on his or her behalf. The same procedure will be used, only this time the roles are reversed in that the witnesses will be examined-in-chief by the respondent's lawyer, followed by cross-examination by the applicant's lawyer, with re-examination, if necessary, by the respondent's lawyer.

REPLY EVIDENCE

Occasionally evidence is given by a witness for the respondent that raises new issues not dealt with by the applicant in the initial presentation of its case. In these circumstances, the applicant may be permitted to call "reply" witnesses to address any new issues raised by the respondent's case.

SUBMISSIONS

After the witnesses have testified, counsel will usually be given an opportunity to "make submissions," or argument to the court, based on the evidence that has been presented. The argument may consist of highlighting the evidence that particularly supports the client's version of the facts and challenging the assertions of the opposing party. This is the time (apart from arguments about the admissibility of specific evidence during the trial) that the lawyers may refer to other judicial precedents in trying to convince the court to interpret the law in their client's favour. If a novel point of law is raised during the case, the judge may occasionally request that the lawyers prepare written submissions and may adjourn the case to allow for preparation time.

JUDGEMENT

After all the evidence has been received and the lawyers' arguments made, the judge must decide the case. Sometimes the judge will be ready to decide the case immediately or after a brief adjournment to consider the matter "in chambers" (the judge's office). In other cases, the judge will "reserve judgement" and adjourn to a future date when the decision will be released. Contrary to popular belief, judges do not routinely have transcripts of the evidence prepared. They rely for the most part upon their own recollection of the evidence, their own notes and the pleadings and written documents that were admitted as exhibits in the trial. The judge may need time to consider the evidence in the case or to review the law in the area. One of the critical functions of a trial judge is to determine the credibility and weight to be attributed to the various witnesses heard throughout the trial.

Most decisions are given orally, although they are recorded by the court reporter so that they can be subsequently transcribed at the request of a party. Sometimes, either because the lawyers have requested it or because the judge decides that the issues warrant it, the judge will prepare a written decision that will be read and distributed to the parties at the judgement date.

If the case deals with an important legal issue or a unique factual situation, the written judgement may be "reported" in a computerized data base or may later appear in a public "law report" so that it may be accessible to lawyers and other judges. In child protection cases and criminal prosecutions involving young offenders or allegations of child abuse by a family member, the reports will give only the initials of the parties so as to protect the privacy of children and non-offending parents. In some provinces, such as Quebec, all family law cases are reported by number, so as to protect family privacy. In most provinces, however, the identity of the parties to a divorce may be revealed in reports of the case.

A NOTE ON CRIMINAL TRIALS

The conducting of a criminal trial is in many ways similar to a civil trial, although the proceedings tend to be more formal, especially if there is a jury. In Canada, civil cases (divorce and child protection) involving children are always decided by a judge sitting without a jury, but the most serious criminal charges may be resolved by a jury trial, even if there are child witnesses.

A criminal case is commenced by means of a very short written statement setting out the charges, known as an information or indictment. There are no pleadings setting out the position of the parties. Unless the accused is prepared to admit certain facts, the Crown is obliged to establish and prove all matters related to the offence in court, without any significant background information. As a result of this and other factors related to the more formal criminal process, criminal trials often last longer than civil cases.

In a criminal trial, the Crown always calls its witnesses first, followed by the defence witnesses, if there are any. If the Crown does not prove all of the elements of its case through its evidence, the lawyer for the accused may ask to have the case dismissed without calling any evidence. The lawyers in a criminal case also make submissions to the court, following which a verdict is rendered.

Criminal trials are usually open to the public, although the Crown may request that the public be excluded if there is a child witness.

If an accused is found guilty, the sentencing will usually take place on another date, after the court considers any additional evidence presented either by the Crown or the defence counsel that relates to the kind of sentence that is appropriate. If a period of imprisonment is being considered, the judge may request that a pre-sentence report be prepared by a probation worker before sentencing.

HIGHLIGHTS OF CHAPTER 4

This chapter outlined the normal process of a civil case. Some of the important points to remember are:

- The lawyer for the applicant (or party asking the court to make an order) presents its witnesses first.

- After the lawyer for the applicant examines a witness "in chief," the lawyer for the respondent (or party responding) may cross-examine the witness.

- The respondent then calls his or her witnesses, who are cross-examined by the applicant.

- If new issues are raised by the respondent, the applicant may be permitted to call evidence in reply after the respondent's evidence is heard.

- After all the evidence is heard, the applicant's lawyer makes submissions about the evidence and the law, followed by the lawyer for the respondent.

- The judge makes a decision, either at the completion of submissions or at a later date.

- The trial process in a criminal case is similar to a civil trial, with the Crown calling its evidence first. The accused may testify and call witnesses but is not obliged to do so.

CHAPTER 5

THE RULES OF EVIDENCE

This chapter will explore the most important rules of evidence, which determine what a court can properly consider in the course of a trial to decide the facts of a case. The following discussion will provide only an introduction to a set of topics often found to be complex and contentious by lawyers, judges and legal scholars.

Trial judges frequently have significant discretion in how they apply these rules. The rules of evidence tend to be more strictly applied in criminal proceedings than in the civil courts. It is not uncommon in a civil case involving the welfare of a child for the parties to agree to waive the application of some of the rules of evidence to simplify the proceedings, and to ensure that the judge has all the information available to make the best decision about a child.

It is important to emphasize that the application of the rules of evidence in practice may differ from the introductory discussion here. It is nevertheless useful to have a general understanding of the rules of evidence, as this may affect how a professional investigates or deals with a case in the community as well as affecting court proceedings.

ISSUES OF FACT AND ISSUES OF LAW

In a trial, the court must determine what actually transpired by making findings of fact. Once the facts are determined, the court must apply the law to determine the consequences that ought to follow from the facts as proven. Where a judge hears a case without a jury, the judge will determine the facts and apply the law.

In serious criminal cases, the accused may choose to have a jury trial. The judge determines the legal issues about the admissibility of the evidence the jury will receive and instructs the jury about the applicable law. The jury is responsible for assessing the evidence and for deciding whether the Crown has proven, beyond a reasonable doubt, that the accused is guilty.

RELEVANCE

It is a requirement that all evidence, whether oral testimony, documents or tapes, be relevant to the issues of a case. Sometimes in a trial, lawyers will engage in heated debate over the relevance of a particular piece of evidence. For example, evidence of spousal violence may be brought before the court by a child protection agency as relevant to the finding that a child is in need of protection. The parents' lawyer might argue that the evidence relating to an incident of marital conflict should not be considered if there is no suggestion that the child was in any way assaulted by the parents. The lawyer for the child protection agency, on the other hand, might be expected to argue that the fact of spousal violence is directly related to the emotional well-being of the child and that the existence of violent episodes between the parents places the child at risk of physical harm as well as emotional harm. The judge ultimately decides the issue of relevance. As we shall see, some evidence that may be relevant may nevertheless be deemed inadmissible.

WEIGHT AND ADMISSIBILITY OF EVIDENCE

The law distinguishes between issues of "admissibility" and "weight" of evidence. Admissibility refers to whether a piece of evidence (such as an aspect of a witness's testimony) should even be considered by the court. udges decide, based on the laws of evidence, whether particular evidence should be "admitted." Issues of admissibility typically arise only if raised by a party. If no party objects, judges are usually quite flexible about the admission of evidence, especially in civil cases. If objections are raised, the judge must apply the laws of evidence to decide whether the evidence is admissible.

It is sometimes necessary to conduct a "hearing within the hearing" in order to review the evidence itself before making a decision as to its admissibility. This is called a *voir dire* (a corruption of an ancient French expression meaning "to hear the truth"), and it occurs in the absence of the jury if there is one.

One of the tasks of the judge or jury is to determine how much "weight," or consideration, is to be given to different pieces of admissible evidence. At the end of the presentation of all of the evidence, lawyers make "submissions," summarizing their case and arguing about the law relevant to issues deciding the case. The lawyers will often suggest to the court which evidence they believe should be accorded greater weight, and why. Likewise, the lawyers will argue about evidence that they believe should not be given much weight for various reasons. For example, a professional opinion based entirely upon second-hand information would not be given as much weight as evidence based upon several intensive interviews with the parties. The testimony of a witness who has revealed a strong bias or whose recollection of events is vague might also be discounted by the court.

In civil child-related proceedings, judges often deal with arguments about the admissibility or reliability of evidence by saying they will admit it as evidence but the concerns expressed will "go to its weight," i.e., it will be received, but given limited consideration. Issues of admissibility of evidence are usually more contentious in criminal cases, where the rules of evidence are stricter and evidence is more likely to be ruled inadmissible.

PREJUDICE AND FAIRNESS

Judges have the discretion to exclude evidence that is considered more prejudicial than probative. In a criminal case, for example, a judge may decide to prohibit cross-examination of an accused about aspects of his criminal record if the judge is concerned that a jury might unfairly infer that the accused is guilty merely because she or he has a criminal record. Judges are most likely to preclude cross-examination on a prior record if the offence occurred some time in the past.[17]

Where the welfare of a child is at stake in civil cases, a judge will tend to take a more liberal approach to the rules of evidence. The judge will be concerned with having as much evidence as possible on which to base a decision about the child's future. Even in these cases, however, a judge may restrict questioning about issues that are likely to be embarrassing and do not seem relevant to the parents' present ability to care for a child.

TYPES OF EVIDENCE

Oral Testimony

Oral testimony (sometimes referred to as *viva voce*, which is Latin for "live voice") evidence refers to evidence given orally by witnesses who testify on the stand.

Most witnesses swear an oath prior to giving testimony in order to ensure the truthfulness of their evidence. For those of the Christian faith, the oath is sworn on the Bible. It is possible to swear an oath on holy books other than the Bible, however. A Moslem may testify by giving an oath on the Koran, or a Jew on the Torah. For those witnesses who are uncomfortable with swearing an oath, the law permits a solemn affirmation instead. This is a statement that the witness solemnly affirms (i.e., promises) that all that will be said is true. An oath and a solemn affirmation are legally equivalent.

A witness must be competent (not suffering from incapacity due to age or mental impairment). Young children may testify without an oath or affirmation. The *Canada Evidence Act* provides that children in criminal cases may testify if the judge is satisfied that they have "the ability to communicate" in court, and they are prepared to "promise to tell the truth." Generally speaking, witnesses can only testify about what they themselves saw, heard or experienced.

---

[17] *R. v. Corbett,* [1988] 1 S.C.R. 670.

Documentary Evidence

Documentary evidence usually refers to any piece of evidence in written form, such as letters, reports, hospital records, certificates and so forth. Also included are affidavits (statements prepared in writing and sworn before a lawyer, Justice of the Peace or commissioner of oaths). Affidavits are sometimes prepared in advance of a hearing either because a witness is unavailable at the time of trial or in order to expedite the trial by eliminating the need to testify in-chief.

Historically, all documentary evidence was prohibited on the grounds that it was hearsay (see "Hearsay," page 78) unless the author was available in court for cross-examination. Over the years, most jurisdictions have enacted legislation to permit the admission of certain types of documentary evidence, so long as fair notice has been given to the other parties. Despite the "relaxing" of the traditional rules of evidence, in the case of medical, hospital and business records, it is sometimes successfully argued by opposing counsel that the authors of those documents should be made available at court for cross-examination on perceptions and opinions stated within the records.

If a party to litigation claims to have a document but fails to produce it without a good expanation, the court may infer that the document never existed. This is sometimes called "the best evidence rule," as the court wants the document itself rather than a claim that it exists.

Real and Demonstrative Evidence

These categories of evidence include those that are either directly related to the facts alleged, in that they are the specific objects referred to, or they are pieces of evidence that demonstrate or illustrate one or more of the issues in dispute. Examples are photographs, charts, maps, anatomically correct dolls, models, demonstrations, videotapes, belts, wires, cords and so on.

If there is any question as to admissibility, any party who objects has the right to present arguments to the court as to why a given object should not be considered. For example, in a jury trial it might be argued that the admission of coloured photographs of an abused child would be too "prejudicial" to the accused.

EXCLUSIONARY RULES OF EVIDENCE

Apart from eliminating evidence that is not relevant to the proceedings, our courts have developed rules to control the quality of evidence that can come before a court. Relevant evidence that is excluded by a rule of law is said to be "inadmissible."

The Hearsay Rule

The hearsay rule can be stated as follows: "A statement other than made by a person while giving oral evidence in the proceedings is inadmissible as evidence of any fact stated."[18]

Because the originator of the out-of-court statement (the so-called "declarant") is not under oath and is not available to be cross-examined on precisely what was said or meant by the statement in question, the statement is excluded from consideration in a court of law as evidence to support its truth. Hearsay can be found in written documents as well as oral testimony.

A statement that appears to be hearsay can be considered by a court so long as it is not being offered to prove the truth of its contents. For example, if a child's teacher stated in court, regarding one of her pupils, that "Jane told me that her father said if she told anyone, he'd kill her," that statement would be hearsay and might be inadmissible in establishing that Jane's father had in fact threatened to harm her. It might, however, be admitted in evidence as explaining why the teacher contacted the child protection authorities.

In proceedings that are "on consent" or not opposed by any of the parties, it is routine to submit evidence that contains hearsay evidence. Even in contested matters, it is not uncommon for the lawyers to agree that certain "hearsay" evidence will be admitted on a "consent" basis, especially where the particular facts are not

---

[18] Rupert Cross, *Evidence,* 7th ed. (London: Butterworths, 1990), 42. For a detailed review of the laws of evidence relevant to protection proceedings, see D.A.R. Thompson, Chapter 13, "Rules of Evidence and Preparing for Court," in Bala, Hornick and Vogl, eds., *Canadian Child Welfare Law* (Toronto: Thompson Educational Publishing, 1991), 263. One of the most accessible legal texts in the area is David Paciocco and Lee Stuesser, *The Law of Evidence,* 2d ed. (Toronto: Irwin Law, 1999).

in dispute. Where a matter is hotly contested, lawyers will often object vigorously to evidence on the grounds that it is hearsay.

Exceptions to the Hearsay Rule: Statutory and Common Law

Like many legal rules, the hearsay rule has evolved over time to accommodate some exceptions. Most of these exceptions reflect situations in which it may be necessary to accept the hearsay evidence, as it would be very difficult or impossible to obtain the evidence otherwise, and in circumstances where the concerns that gave rise to the rule are substantially reduced because there is some assurance of the reliability of the out-of-court statements.

Legislatures have decided that, for practical reasons, in some circumstances the hearsay rule must be relaxed. Most jurisdictions, for example, have enacted statutes that help to facilitate the admission of documents without the necessity of calling every person who has ever made a notation on an official record. A number of exceptions to the hearsay rule have also been developed by judges as part of the common law.

Business Records

In most jurisdictions, the legislature has allowed for the routine admission into evidence of records that are defined as "business records." Section 35 of *the Ontario Evidence Act* defines "business" to include "every kind of business, profession, occupation, calling, operation or activity, whether carried on for profit or otherwise." Examples of records that regularly fall into the definition of "business records" are hospital records and school records.

The legislation allows for the admission of any writing or record of any transaction, occurrence or event, provided that it occurred in the "ordinary and usual course" of the operation, and that it was in the "ordinary and usual course" of the procedure of the operation of the establishment that the writing or record was made. Even though it is not necessary to have the person who originally made the record present in court, it is necessary to have some person present to testify and explain from personal knowledge how the records are made and to satisfy the judge that they were made "in the usual and ordinary" course of the operation.

In Ontario, the legislation requires seven days notice to be given to the other parties where a party wishes to ask that a business record be admitted into evidence. The other parties are entitled to review the documents before the court considers their admission into evidence.

While some Canadian judges are prepared to admit child protection agency files as "business records" in contested child protection cases, many judges are not prepared to do this and require agency workers to testify and be available for cross-examination.

Official Documents

For documents such as court orders, judgements, birth certificates, certificates of conviction and other government documents, legislation generally allows the filing of a certificate or sealed copy without having any person attest to their accuracy.

Medical and Psychological Reports

Governments have been sensitive to the difficulties that the court process can create for doctors and certain other health professionals. Doctors and psychologists are very busy professionals whose time is in great demand, and legislation permits, in specified circumstances, a medical or psychological report to be received by a court without the author having to testify.

A medical report might be a simple letter on the doctor's letterhead, or an extensive report of medical findings. Usually a report prepared by a medical practitioner duly qualified to practice in Canada can be admitted without the doctor being present in court. The other parties must have at least 10 days' notice of the fact that a report will be filed and may inspect the report prior to the trial. If the other parties wish the opportunity to cross-examine the doctor, they have the right to insist on this. If the doctor has been forced to attend court unnecessarily, however, the party insisting on his or her presence may be responsible for the cost of the doctor's attendance at court. In Ontario, since 1989, a report by a registered psychologist has been admissible in the same fashion as a medical report.

A medical or psychological report that is written for a case that may be contested should be accurate, detailed and fair. If the report is incomplete, inaccurate or lacking in balance, it may undermine the credibility of the author. In contested cases, lawyers will often require the author of a medical or psychological report to attend court as a witness, particularly where the information in the report is of questionable reliability or if the professionals involved have different opinions about the case.

Common Law Exceptions to the Hearsay Rule

Judges have articulated a number of exceptions to the hearsay rule.

Admissions by a Party

If a witness relates a statement made out of court by a person who is a party to the proceedings, the statement will generally be admitted into evidence. As an example, in a case involving allegations of abuse by a parent, a teacher would be permitted to testify about statements made to the teacher by that parent about the injury to the child.

This exception to the hearsay rule is based on the fact that the usual concerns regarding hearsay evidence are alleviated by the presence of the originator of the statement as a party in the court. A party who is present can take the stand to deny the statement if it is false, or offer a context for the statement if it is true. Also, this exception is based upon the notion that a statement by a party against his or her interest has certain inherent trustworthiness. People rarely lie to hurt themselves, but rather to help themselves.

When a witness testifies about the admission of a party, statements must be given in context so that the court is not misled. Accordingly, the witness may be requested to relate the entire conversation in which the statement was made.

In criminal cases, statements made by the accused to a "person-in-authority" will only be admissible if they satisfy the "confession rule." Such statements must be "voluntary," in that they must be made voluntarily and without improper inducements or threats. The "confession rule" applies to any statement made to a "person-in-authority," which is defined as a person whom the accused would reasonably believe is in a position to influence the prosecution of the case. Police officers are always regarded as persons-in-authority and must exercise considerable care in taking statements from accused persons.

"Confessions" by accused individuals to persons-in-authority may also be ruled inadmissible if taken in violation of section 10 of the *Charter of Rights*. This section requires that a person who has been arrested by the police must be advised of the right to consult with counsel before making a statement, and that he or she is under no obligation to answer questions. There are special, additional protections for young persons (aged 12 through 17) charged under the *Young Offenders Act*; their statements are particularly closely scrutinized by the courts to ensure voluntariness and to protect their rights. The court looks at whether the youth was allowed to consult with a parent and a lawyer before deciding to make a statement.

In most situations a statement made by a suspect or by a person who has been charged to a social worker or teacher will be admissible. In certain circumstances, a teacher or social worker might be viewed as a "person-in-authority," and so it is possible that a statement made to them is inadmissible in a criminal prosecution (unless the suspect is properly advised of his legal rights). Until the police have completed their interrogation of a suspected abuser where a criminal prosecution is contemplated, other professionals should normally avoid interviewing the suspect. The police are responsible for ensuring that a suspect's legal rights are respected before a statement is taken, and that any statement that is given is legally admissible. Beyond concerns about the protection of legal rights and the admissibility of any statement, the police receive special training in the interrogation of suspects and understandably do not want the investigations of crimes complicated by the prior involvement of others.

Accusations Made in the Presence of a Party

In addition to statements of a party, statements that are made in the presence and hearing of a party may be admitted in court. Take, for example, an accusation by a mother in the presence of the father that he had assaulted their child. The father might have admitted the statement by his words or reaction, such as a nod, acknowledging the statement to be true. If the father remained silent, the court might infer that the statement were true if it would be otherwise reasonable to deny it. In these circumstances, a person hearing the accusation (such as a neighbour) can repeat both the statement and the response of the father, so long as it has been established that the accusation was heard by the father.

"Necessity" and "Reliability": Children's Disclosures of Abuse

In an important 1990 decision, *R. v. Khan,*[19] the Supreme Court of Canada ruled that judges should have a flexible approach to the admission of hearsay. They should be prepared to receive such evidence where there is a "necessity" for doing so and where the statements appear to have "reliability." In *Khan,* the Supreme Court ruled that the mother of a three-and-one-half-year-old child (who was considered too young to testify) should be permitted to testify about a graphic disclosure of abuse made shortly after the alleged abuse, even though the statement was hearsay.

The Supreme Court seemed sensitive to some of the difficulties inherent in a child sexual abuse prosecution, suggesting that hearsay statements might be admissible instead of a child's testimony if the statements were "reliable" and testifying would be "traumatic ... or harm the child." The "reliability" of a statement, for these purposes, is to be determined by the circumstances of the disclosure, including such factors as the child's age and demeanour, the situation of the disclosure and whether there are reasonable grounds to suspect fabrication. The "necessity" arises from the need to prevent further trauma to the child or from the

---

[19] [1990] 2 S.C.R. 531.

fact that the child is considered too young to testify, so hearsay statements must be received instead of the child's testimony.

In some cases involving disclosures of allegations of abuse to a person such as a teacher, the person to whom a child discloses the abuse may be able to testify about the disclosures *in addition to having the child testify*. This makes it especially important for any person to whom a disclosure of abuse is made to make full notes about exactly what was said immediately after the disclosure to ensure that the court receives a full and fair report.[20]

While the jurisprudence is still evolving, the result of *Khan* is that children, especially younger children, may not always have to testify in sexual abuse prosecutions. However, Crown Attorneys still feel that cases in which a child is unable to testify are more difficult to successfully prosecute.

Even if the child's disclosure is not admissible in a criminal case, it may be admissible in a civil case or may assist the police or child protection workers in investigating a case. It is generally somewhat easier to prove abuse in a civil custody or child protection proceeding than in a criminal trial, and judges in civil cases are more willing to admit the hearsay statements of a child.

Counselling Records of a Victim of Sexual Offences

Often defence counsel will attempt to access information in counselling or other records containing personal information about a victim. The *Criminal Code* requires the defence counsel to serve a Notice of Application on the person in control of the records as well as the Crown Attorney. The accused must establish that production of the records is necessary in the interests of justice. At the first stage, the accused must satisfy the judge that the records contain information relevant to an issue at trial or to the competence of a witness.

It is not sufficient to establish that the record exists or that it may relate to the credibility of the complainant (in other words, it cannot be a "fishing expedition"). Even where the accused can discharge the preliminary onus, the court may order that the

---

[20] See, for example, *R. v. B. (D.C.)* (1994), 32 C.R. (4th) 91 (Man. C.A.).

records be produced and reviewed by the judge. The judge must then make a determination as to what, if any, of the material contained in the records, when weighed against society's interest in respecting the privacy and dignity of the victim, is nonetheless necessary to be produced to counsel in order for the accused to make a full answer and defence. The judge may decide to disclose only those portions of the record most relevant to the proceedings.

Opinion Evidence

Generally, a witness is not entitled to express an opinion or a conclusion about the facts at issue. The witness can usually only state the facts directly seen or heard by the witness, and leaves the court to draw the appropriate inferences.

For example, a social worker from a child protection agency who is concerned about the psychiatric state of a client might not be permitted to offer an opinion as to the psychiatric diagnosis of that client (e.g., that the client appeared to be "psychotic") but would be entitled to describe in detail the observations that would allow the court to draw inferences about the client's mental state (e.g., "Mrs. J. did not appear to hear my questions. She was gazing at the corner, and crying out that the neighbours were laughing at her through the walls, and asked if I could hear them. I could not hear any noise coming from beyond the apartment wall.").

There are, however, two exceptions to the rule regarding opinion evidence.

1. A witness may be asked to express an opinion on matters of general knowledge about which any person can and does have an opinion (i.e., sobriety, demonstration of affection). In the above example, a judge might allow the witness to express an opinion in a general way about the psychiatric or mental state of the client, so long as it does not extend to a medical or psychiatric diagnosis ("I was concerned about Mrs. J's perception of reality and her mental state at that moment.").

2. If the witness has been established as an "expert" as a result of training or experience in the field in which his or her opinion is being solicited (e.g., a psychiatrist or social worker who has specialized training in a given field), the witness may give "expert opinion" testimony.

When faced with competing arguments from counsel about whether the witness is qualified to offer an opinion on a given subject, a judge in a civil case will sometimes permit the witness to offer the opinion and then determine the appropriate weight to be placed on that opinion based upon the whole of the witness's testimony.

Even where a witness has outstanding credentials to qualify his or her opinion as expert, the court is not bound to accept the conclusions of that witness. (For a further discussion on opinion evidence, see "Testifying as an Expert," page 109).

The Supreme Court of Canada has begun to restrict the extent to which it will permit mental health professionals to testify in criminal cases about the symptoms of child abuse and the extent to which a child's behaviour is consistent with abuse.[21] There is a concern that criminal trials may become long, expensive "battles of experts," which may be unfair to accused persons who often cannot afford to retain their own experts.

Privilege

A witness who is subpoenaed to court must not only attend but, generally speaking, must answer all proper questions put to him or her. The refusal to answer may be considered contempt of court and could result in a fine or even imprisonment.

While the truth-seeking objectives of the courtroom are extremely important, the law has come to recognize that occasionally there are competing social values that may justify a witness's reluctance to answer. The term *privilege* refers to the right that a person may have to prevent the release of certain information to the court.

---

[21] *R. v. D.D.*, [2000] SCC 43.

Some of the kinds of privilege acknowledged in our legal system are

- *the privilege against self-incrimination*: the accused is not required to testify against her or himself;
- *spousal privilege*: the rule that one spouse can not be forced to give testimony against the other in a criminal prosecution. This privilege has been abolished in relation to offences involving abuse of children by the 1988 amendments to the *Criminal Code* (Bill C-15);
- *professional privilege*: most commonly, the privilege between a solicitor and client. This privilege is based on the notion that without the assurance of complete confidentiality, the effectiveness of our legal system would be greatly impaired. The privilege extends not only to what a client says to the lawyer but to the notes and records kept by the lawyer and even to reports produced in preparation for court. For example, if a lawyer sends the client to a psychiatrist to obtain a report as to the client's psychiatric status, neither the psychiatrist nor the lawyer can be compelled to reveal the contents of the report.

In rare circumstances, courts have been willing to acknowledge a limited privilege between other professionals and their clients or patients, such as clergymen, doctors and social workers. In Canada, to date, however, the only absolute professional privilege is between a solicitor and client.

Video and Audiotapes

Video and audiotapes are being used more and more, particularly in sexual abuse cases where the critical evidence is the statement of the child about the abuse. The courts have traditionally been cautious in admitting video and audiotapes into evidence. However, the *Criminal Code* was amended in 1988 (Bill C-15) to allow videotaped statements made by children to be admitted in prosecutions under the following certain circumstances:

- the child victim must be under the age of 18 at the time the videotape is made;
- the tape must be made "within a reasonable time" after the alleged offence;
- the child must "adopt" the contents of the tape (i.e., the child must be a witness in court while the tape is played, be specifically questioned about whether it is accurate and be available to be cross-examined on the contents by defence counsel).

While the provisions do not eliminate the need for children to testify in court, they have the potential to alleviate some of the problems created by the long delays between the time of disclosure and trial. Even where a videotape is not tendered in evidence, it may be useful for refreshing the memory of a child before testifying. Further, experience in the United States indicates that some abusers plead guilty after viewing a videotape of the child's statement of the abuse.

Despite the provisions of the *Criminal Code* permitting the use of videotapes made in the investigation of child sexual abuse, the trial judge has the discretion to edit or to refuse to admit videotaped evidence where its prejudicial effect outweighs its probative value or, in other words, where the harm to the accused is greater than the potential benefit of the evidence in proving a fact in issue.[22]

In civil proceedings, videotapes in which a child describes an incident or incidents of sexual abuse have sometimes been used *instead* of the child testifying in court.

Often it is a joint team of a police officer and a child protection worker who participate in the making of an audio or videotape of a child's statement for investigative purposes. In a therapeutic or clinical setting, however, another professional may make audio or videotapes that might contain potential evidence in a case involving abuse or neglect. While these tapes are not always admissible in a criminal case, they are sometimes used, often by

---

[22]   In *R. v. L.(D.O.)*, [1993] 4 S.C.R. 419, 85 C.C.C. (3d) 289. *Criminal Code*, s.715.1.

expert witnesses, as evidence in a civil case to illustrate the basis of the opinion offered or for other purposes.

There is considerable judicial discretion as to whether to admit a videotape in a civil proceeding. Judges in Ontario are far from uniform in their treatment of such issues. However, in some provinces, such as Nova Scotia and Saskatchewan, legislation provides for the admission of videotapes of a child's statement in civil cases, instead of having the child testify.

A video or audiotape may be offered in evidence because it contains a statement made, not by the child, but by a parent or other party to the proceedings. For example, if a parent makes an admission in the context of a therapy session with a psychiatrist (e.g., "Yeah, sometimes I hit her. But only when she asks for it."), the tape might be offered as evidence. The parent's lawyer might argue, however, that the statement was privileged and that it should not be revealed by the interviewer without his or her client's express consent. It would be up to the court to determine whether or not the contents of the tape could be admitted in evidence. In civil abuse cases, normally the courts are reluctant to exclude evidence on the basis of "privilege."

The use of videotapes raises some unique challenges to those who wish to make use of them in the courtroom. Counsel for an alleged abuser may object to the admissibility of videotapes or the weight to be given to them on the following types of grounds:

- the interview technique was unsatisfactory; for example, the cross-examining lawyer might try to establish that the way in which the questions were put to the child suggested an answer or led the child to provide the answers given;
- the circumstances of the interview (including the presence of key adults before or during the interview) influenced the contents of the interview;
- the quality of the tape;
- problems in the "continuity" of the possession of the tape from the time of making through to the trial, and the possibilities of damage, erasure, editing and so on.

These are issues that are seriously debated in criminal courts. All persons interviewing children should be trained, should keep detailed records of discussions with the child before and after videotapings, and should ensure that the equipment is operating satisfactorily before conducting the interview.

The development of protocols for the making and storage of audio and videotapes should go a long way towards reducing the problems outlined above, especially where they are made for investigative purposes.

If a tape is made by the police or child protection workers, its contents will normally have to be disclosed to opposing counsel in advance of trial, even if the Crown or the child protection agency does not intend to use the tape in court. With the opportunity to study the child as a prospective witness at close range, the result may be a more penetrating cross-examination or it may produce a guilty plea or a settled case. If a videotape is disclosed to the lawyer for the accused, steps must be taken to ensure that it is not misused. The accused should not be permitted to take the tape home where it might be shown to friends. The Crown Attorney's office usually requires the signing of an Undertaking not to misuse the tape before allowing an accused or his or her counsel to view the tape.

If you plan to use audio or videotapes as the basis of your opinion or as an adjunct to your testimony in court, it will be important for you to know in advance whether any of the counsel will be opposing their admission. If you are being called by the Crown in a case or by the lawyer representing a child protection agency, be sure to consult that lawyer regarding the use of tapes.

Professionals who regularly videotape statements in sexual abuse cases would be well advised to consult the Crown Attorney's office concerning this practice, in order to ensure that tapes will be admissible in subsequent cases. It should be appreciated that any video or audiotape of a child's statement or interview will likely have to be disclosed to an accused person prior to trial and may potentially be used to point out inconsistencies in the child's statement, even if the prosecution does not wish to submit the tape as evidence.

HIGHLIGHTS OF CHAPTER 5

This chapter reviewed the rules that govern what evidence a court will consider in making a decision. Some of the important points to remember are:

- Evidence must be relevant to the issues before the court.

- A judge must decide what evidence should be admitted, and the trier of fact (judge or jury) must decide how much weight to give the evidence.

- Evidence may be excluded if its probative value is outweighed by its prejudicial effect.

- A court may consider evidence that is given orally by witnesses or is contained in documents or through other exhibits, such as photographs.

- If a party objects, "third-party" statements made to a witness are often excluded as "hearsay."

- There are a number of exceptions to the hearsay rule, such as business and hospital records, medical reports, statements made by the parties and in situations of "necessary and reliable" statements of a child, particularly relating to allegations of abuse or neglect.

- In most cases, only a witness with expertise can offer an expert opinion to the court.

- Under the *Criminal Code,* a videotape of a statement by the child victim may be admitted under certain circumstances.

- In civil cases, the rules regarding the admission of audio and videotapes in the courtroom are still developing, but tapes are being admitted more frequently now than in the past.

- A professional who wishes to make an audio or videotape of an investigative interview for use in court should be properly trained about the legal aspects of the taping process.

CHAPTER 6

TESTIFYING IN COURT

I t is often difficult to predict which cases will end up in court in a contested trial, but when the likelihood of future litigation first becomes clear, it is important to take some reasonable steps to maximize your effectiveness as a witness.

START WITH YOUR NOTES

For some professionals, such as police officers or child protection workers, detailed notekeeping in anticipation of court is routine, since arguably all cases should be regarded as potentially going to court. For most other professionals, however, notekeeping, if it is expected, is usually made with objectives quite removed from that of testifying in court.

If you think that a case may end up in court, or in any case where you become aware of a possible incident of child abuse, make complete notes as soon after the event as possible, and sign and date them. By taking a few minutes to write down the details of an incident or observation at the time that it occurs, you will have a record of great assistance to you if you are called upon to testify.

It is wise to keep notes regarding each client or family on separate pages. If you are required to bring your notes to court, information regarding other clients need not be revealed.

YOUR NOTES (FOR TAKING TO THE WITNESS STAND)

The events that stand out so clearly in your mind during the time of a crisis have an unfortunate way of becoming vague recollections over ensuing months. Given that most litigation takes place months if not years following the events in question, the making of notes becomes critical to enhancing the accuracy and therefore the weight to be attributed to your testimony.

Just how much and what sort of information you will need to note will vary according to the nature and circumstances of each case, but the following general guidelines may help professionals.

Contacts with the Child or Caregivers

If possible, note each contact, whether face-to-face (at the office or elsewhere) or by telephone with the child or caregiver. Note the key details of each contact. Some will be routine and uneventful, requiring relatively little detail. Others, because they deal with the issues of abuse or neglect, may require more detailed notation. For example, if you have to note an injury to a child and in the course of your meeting you ask the parent how the injury occurred, every aspect of that interview could be important in a subsequent court hearing. *Some detail in the observations of the injury* (colour, size and so on) and any objective information regarding the degree of pain experienced by the child would be important to note (e.g., the child was holding his left arm and sobbing). If you pose a question to the parent, it is helpful to note to the best of your recollection *the wording of your question and the wording of the answer.*

Likewise, the behaviour of others in the room may also be important evidence in a subsequent hearing. Try to make a note of all persons who were present at the time and record as much detail as you can recall about what was said by each person. It may be important to note accompanying behaviour, facial expressions, gestures, eye movements and so forth, if observed.

For example, the notes of a public health nurse about a visit where she suspected that there may have been physical abuse might resemble the following:

> On my visit of Sept. 17, 2000, I knocked on the door three times, and I heard a voice on the other side of the door, which I recognized as that of Mrs. A, asking who it was. I could also hear the sobbing of a young child. I identified myself, and Mrs. A reluctantly opened the door to allow me to enter. I

> observed Johnny, her seven-year-old son, sobbing and hold-
> ing his left arm. I asked Mrs. A. what had happened to
> Johnny. She stated that he had been playing with his toy car
> on the stairs and had caught his arm in the railing. While she
> recounted this information, she looked downward and did
> not make eye contact with me. Johnny continued to sob qui-
> etly and also looked downward.

By noting the details of the questions, the exact answers and the
non-verbal observations of Mrs. A. and Johnny, the public health
nurse helps to create a vivid picture for the court.

Even in circumstances where the explanation offered at the
time of a visit is consistent with the injury that you observe, the
parent may give other persons a different explanation at different
times. It will be helpful, therefore, to note the explanation offered
with as much accuracy as possible so that it can be compared if
necessary to information provided to others.

Your notes can be a "shorthand" of what you have observed.
You are entitled to elaborate upon them and to have a recollection that is independent of them. What is important, however, is
that you have made a notation that reinforces in your own mind
the events you have observed and refers in at least a perfunctory
fashion to *the key aspects of the occurrence.* In the above situation, the
witness's notes might read:

> Sept. 17, '00: H.V. Mrs. A. and J. Knocked 3 X. Could hear
> child sobbing - Mrs. A. reluctantly let me in. Asked what hap-
> pened to J. - Mrs. A. stated that J. was playing on the stairs
> with toy car, and caught arm in the railing. No eye contact. J.
> sobbing throughout, looking downward.

Likewise, if a child discloses an abusive incident to you, it is imperative that you involve the child protection authorities and police as soon as possible so that they can conduct an investigation.

In some situations, however, you may be the first person to
whom a child has disclosed this incident, and you may need to
obtain a reasonable amount of information to enable you to make
a decision as to whether or not there is reportable suspicion of
abuse or neglect. In this case, try to make accurate notes regarding *the circumstances and wording of that disclosure to the best of your*

recollection, any questions you may have asked to facilitate the disclosure and a description of the emotional state and behaviour of the child.

A detailed description of your verbal exchange with the child will also help to avoid allegations that you have improperly coached the child to make the disclosure, or suggested answers to him or her.

Contacts with Other Professionals

In addition to notes about your contacts with the child and family, it is important to include a brief notation regarding your contacts with other professionals (e.g., child protection worker, police and so forth).

Using Your Notes While Testifying

According to common practice, if you wish to use your notes while testifying, it will be necessary for the lawyer who calls you to establish that they are *your own notes, made contemporaneously with the events in question and not subsequently altered in any way.*[23]

There is no absolute rule about the meaning of "contemporaneous," but generally it is advisable to make your notes as soon after the event as possible, when the events are still fresh in your mind.

If your notes are produced by a secretary from dictation, the person who gave the dictation should review the notes after they are typed to ensure their accuracy and initial the notes to indicate that they have been read.[24] This will ensure that they can be used in court. If handwritten notes are typed, they should also be

---

[23] Some Canadian cases have taken a more flexible view, ruling that a witness may use "anything in writing to revive a recollection" and have permitted use of notes made months after the events in question to aid a witness in testifying, or even the use of notes made by another person. See *R. v. Bengert (No.2)* (1980), 15 C.R. (3d) 114 (B.C.C.A.) and *R v. Green* (1994), 32 C.R. (4th) 248 (Ont. Gen. Div.). While these cases appear to be correctly decided, it is probably prudent to follow accepted practice and ensure that notes are made contemporaneously with the events in question.

[24] Technically, a witness does not have to personally make the notes to use them to "refresh memory." However, if the notes are made by someone else, the witness must review them to ensure their accuracy at a time when the memory is still fresh.

reviewed or the original notes kept for the purposes of court testimony.

The process of establishing through questions that notes meet the commonly accepted legal requirements for using notes is usually referred to as "qualification" of the notes. A typical "qualification" of a witness for use of notes might proceed this way:

Questioning lawyer: "When did you next see Mrs. X.?"

Witness: "May I refer to my notes?"

Judge: "Perhaps, counsel, you had better qualify the notes if the witness wishes to refer to them."

Lawyer: "Of course, your Honour." (To the Witness) "Are those your own notes you are referring to?

Witness: "Yes."

Lawyer: "And when were those notes made?"

Witness: "I routinely prepare notes of my visits or interviews immediately after they occur. On rare occasions, I make my notes the day following the visit or interview."

Lawyer: "When did you make them on this occasion?"

Witness: "I made them in the car, immediately following my visit to the home."

Lawyer: "Were the events still fresh in you mind?"

Witness: "Yes. I could remember the details of my visit vividly."

Lawyer: "And since you first made those notes, have you made any additions or deletions?"

Witness: "No."

Judge: "That's fine, counsel. The witness may refer to his [or her] notes."

It is often said that witnesses should use their notes merely to "refresh their memory." Reading from your notes is not an acceptable replacement for an independent recollection of the events in question. If you have used the notes to refresh your memory, cross-examining counsel are free to look at them in order to assist them in cross-examining you. This right of counsel to examine notes arises even if a witness reviewed the notes prior to coming to court to prepare for testifying and does not actually use the notes on the witness stand. A court may occasionally provide a copy of your notes to the cross-examining lawyer to assist in questioning you. In some cases, counsel will have been provided with a copy of your notes either through the disclosure process or by court order (see Chapter 3, page 59).

MEETING WITH THE LAWYERS IN ADVANCE OF COURT

We have already touched upon some of the issues raised by the disclosure of information to counsel before actually testifying from the witness box (see Chapter 3, page 59).

Confidentiality issues aside, there is no question that advance preparation makes for a more effective and less anxiety-provoking experience for the professional (as well as the questioning lawyer).

It is at a meeting with the lawyer who has called you as a witness that you can find out the nature of the case and the issues likely to be raised by the parties in the hearing, and give the lawyer an idea of the type of evidence you can and cannot offer. The interview can serve the function of a "dry run" of your examination-in-chief. While the lawyer is ethically prohibited from telling you the answers you should offer to given questions, it is perfectly permissible for the lawyer to prepare you by alerting you before the hearing to the key issues that you will be asked to address. The lawyer may also indicate the types of questions that are likely to arise in cross-examination.

Even if your evidence will not support the party who is calling you as a witness, or where there is a great deal of acrimony among the parties, it is important to communicate with the counsel who wishes to call you if for no other reason than to establish a mutually convenient time for testifying and to resolve the issue of fees, where appropriate.

In any situation in which the rules of confidentiality do not apply, it is proper to discuss the case with any party or lawyer on the case who contacts you for that purpose. Indeed, the failure to be open with representatives of all of the parties prior to court could adversely affect a professional witness's credibility.

Witnesses are usually entitled to a fee, which varies depending upon the kind of proceeding and whether or not they are testifying as an "expert" in the case (see "Testifying as an Expert" in this chapter, page 109).

Unless you return the lawyer's calls to discuss your availability and the issue of fees, the subpoena or summons may arrive without your input as to preferred date or time, and with a cheque no larger than the minimum required to make it binding in law.

Whether or not you have a meeting beforehand with the lawyer who is calling you as a witness, you should attempt to ascertain as much of the following information as possible:

- What day or days are scheduled for the trial?
- In which court is the case being heard?
- What type of proceeding is involved? (Criminal, child protection, divorce, and so on)
- Are the proceedings open to the public?
- Is there a jury?
- How many parties are there? Are they all represented? Who is representing the other parties?
- Who is bringing the matter before the court?
- What are the issues that are likely to arise? What is the position of each of the parties with respect to those issues?
- What other witnesses are expected to testify?
- What issues in particular are you being called upon to address?
- What information will you be called upon to share?

- Will you be asked to render an expert opinion on any of those issues?
- What time will you be required to be available at court?
- Is it possible for you to be "on call" for court at your office, or do you need to be waiting at the court house?

Written Summary

If you meet with the lawyer before the hearing, it is useful to prepare in advance a written summary that can serve as the basis of your interview, as well as prepare you for your testimony. It is helpful to bring two copies of your summary with you so that you can leave one with the lawyer for his or her file. Generally, notes or a summary prepared just before court cannot be used by a witness to assist in testifying, although many witnesses find such notes very useful in organizing their thoughts about a case beforehand. As discussed above, it is common practice that only notes prepared "contemporaneously" with the events in question can be used while testifying to "refresh the memory" of a witness. If you prepare a written summary, it should contain:

1. *The context of your involvement.* Prepare a brief summary of the general context of your involvement; for example, "I have been teaching at the primary level at Riverside Public School for the past five years, since I graduated in 1996. For the past two years, I have been Johnny's teacher while he has been in Grade 3 and Grade 4."

2. *A summary of your contacts.* This would include the information in your notes (as discussed earlier).

3. *Your opinions.* (See "Opinion Evidence," page 85; see also "Testifying as an Expert" in this chapter, page 109.) If you are an "expert" in a relevant area (e.g., medical doctor, psychologist and so on), summarize any areas in which you have formulated opinions that may be relevant to the issues of the case. Whether or not your opinions will be solicited in the course of your testimony is a judgement call on the part of the lawyer and is subject to the judge accepting your "qualifications."

4. *Questions you have about aspects of your evidence.* Sometimes you will be unsure as to how best to present certain aspects of your evidence. For example, you may wish to clarify whether a certain statement is "hearsay" or whether it will be considered admissible as an exception to the hearsay rule.

A witness should not be overly concerned with whether or not all of the evidence he or she has to offer is admissible. It is best to give the lawyer an unedited version of the testimony that you want to give and let the lawyer worry about admissibility. (See Chapter 5, "The Rules of Evidence," page 73).

5. *Any other information.* Sometimes you are aware of other potential witnesses who may not have come to the attention of the lawyer but who have relevant information to offer to the court. This could be particularly important in a criminal or child protection case, where the Crown or lawyer representing the child protection agency has a duty to ensure that the evidence fully and fairly reflects the case before the court. If you have such information, it is best to contact the Crown or lawyer immediately due to the requirement that such evidence be disclosed to the other side in a timely fashion.

6. *Your up-to-date curriculum vitae.* Your curriculum vitae may be important to help establish your qualifications as an "expert witness."

WRITING REPORTS FOR COURT

Frequently, professionals such as doctors or psychologists are requested by one or more parties to prepare a written report of their involvement for court purposes. A written report can be useful in the following ways:

- It prepares the professional for the possibility of testifying by necessitating a review of the contacts with the parties and opinions about the case.

- It provides the parties with a concrete summary for purposes of disclosure and negotiation. If the parties can come to an agreement, the report may be submitted with the consent of all parties and without the necessity of a court appearance.
- In many cases, the parties will accept the report without requiring the author to testify; dispensing with oral testimony is most likely to occur if the report is fair, accurate and complete.
- If a court appearance is necessary, the report serves as a focus for testimony.

When writing a report for court, consider who might be likely to read it. Any report that is to be used in court will have to be shared with all the parties. When a copy is provided to a party's lawyer, it is generally the responsibility of that lawyer to review its content with the client.

Be sure to give the parties ample time to consider your report before the court date. There are statutory requirements for advance filing of reports. Sometimes a report cannot be filed in evidence at all because it does not fall into the specific provisions of the evidence statute. If a report is shared in advance with opposing counsel, however, it may be admitted on a consent basis even if the statutory notice requirements are not fully satisfied.

Counsel always has the right to require the author of a report to come to court to testify and to be subjected to cross-examination. (See "Business Records" and also "Medical and Psychological Reports," pages 79-80, in Chapter 5.)

A useful court report should provide the information suggested above in the written summary for court (context of involvement, summary of contacts, opinions, curriculum vitae). As is the case with oral testimony, a report is enhanced by accuracy and specificity. Be as specific as you can about the date, time and length of a visit, interview or examination. Be sure to include who was present and the location of the meeting.

Where it is necessary to refer to information received from third parties, try to set out clearly the information that has been reported to you and its source. Thus, if the parties wish to omit the information *or* request the court to ignore it, it can be easily distinguished from your own observations and opinions.

Likewise, be sure to set out your opinions and formulations separately from the facts and observations so that the court is free to "check out" the reasonableness of your conclusions as measured against the objective information you have offered.

When offering an opinion, it is wise to back it up by referring specifically to the factual material that has led you to that conclusion. For example, don't simply state that "Mrs. W. has unresolved anger at her mother," but rather explain this conclusion by adding, "This is demonstrated by her descriptions of childhood abuse while in her mother's care, together with a history of conflict with female authority figures."

It is also important to avoid the unnecessary use of professional jargon in a report so that the parties can interpret your report without the necessity of a court appearance. If you need to use a technical term, be sure to offer a lay explanation within the text of the report.

Reports should never be sent directly to the judge unless the judge has requested or ordered the report. Usually reports are directed to the party who has requested them.

EXAMINATION-IN-CHIEF (OR DIRECT EXAMINATION)

Each witness is given an opportunity in answering a series of general questions to offer a narrative to the court summarizing the nature of his or her involvement in a particular case. The lawyer who calls a witness will conduct an examination-in-chief (or direct examination). The rules are quite strict about the types of questions that may be put to a witness during direct examination. During direct examination, the lawyer should not lead the witness.

Leading questions are defined as questions that suggest an answer or presume a fact not in evidence. Often, leading questions are those that seem to invite a "yes" or a "no" answer. For example: "Isn't it true, Ms. W., that this is the worst case of child abuse that you have ever seen?" Such a question would be perfectly permissible during cross-examination but is unacceptable in direct, since it seems to put words into the mouth of the witness. Sometimes, if the lawyer in direct examination knows what evidence the witness has to give, questions can be rephrased without offending the rules regarding leading questions. "Can you comment upon the seriousness of this particular case of abuse based upon your experience in the field, Ms. W.?" would be a non-leading way of eliciting the same evidence from the expert witness.

In many situations all counsel will agree to allow the use of leading questions by examining counsel in areas that are relatively non-controversial, such as the qualifications of a witness or the recollection of significant dates. The rules will be strictly enforced, however, where the answers deal with issues that are important to the determination of the case. It is imperative, therefore, to ensure that you answer questions put to you in direct examination as fully as possible.

Questions on examination-in-chief are designed to facilitate your own narrative of the events in question. They might focus your attention on a given date, for example, and then ask you to tell the court what happened.

As you can see, the key to examination-in-chief is preparation, both by yourself and if at all possible in conjunction with the lawyer, so that expectations are clear.

Tips for Coming to Court & Examination-in-Chief

- Look the part. Court is a serious place, and your dress should reflect this. You should be dressed in a professional manner.
- Do not chew gum.
- If you are in the courtroom when the judge enters, stand up until you are told to sit down. Only lawyers bow to the judge as a formal sign of respect when court starts or upon leaving the courtroom; witnesses need not do this. Often a lawyer will remain standing as a way of cueing the judge that the lawyer wishes to address the court.

- Stand up if the judge leaves the courtroom.

- If court is already in session and you are called to testify from outside the courtroom, proceed directly to the witness box.

- If you need water, a chair (if there is none) or any other reasonable amenity, politely request it of the judge before you begin.

- If you require a "comfort" break during the course of your testimony, request it. The court will take regular recesses in any event, usually at a convenient break in the proceedings.

- If you need to address the judge directly, use either "Sir" or "Madam" since the official title may vary according to the specific court you are in. If you have heard the lawyers address the judge as "Your Honour," "Your Worship," "My Lord" or "My Ladyship," you may take your cues from them.

- Speak slowly. Remember that the judge will likely be relying on his or her own handwritten notes of your testimony. Further, a court reporter will be trying to keep a verbatim record. If a transcript is ordered, it will not be a good one if the court reporter has not been able to transcribe all of your evidence.

- Be aware of the tone and modulation of your voice. The courtroom is, after all, a social situation. You need to capture and keep the attention of the judge, jury (if applicable) and lawyers. Use your voice to emphasize important aspects of your testimony. If you are lacking in energy or you lose your train of thought, the effectiveness of your testimony will be lessened.

- Speak loudly and clearly. There is nothing worse than a mumbling witness. Not only is it irritating for those who are sincerely trying to hear what you have to say, but it tends to leave the impression that you are not confident in what you are saying. This can be damaging to your credibility.

- Be aware of your body language. The judge (and jury if there is one) will be watching you throughout your testimony and will be assessing your credibility, not only by what you say, but by the way that you say it. It may be useful to practice testifying in front of a video-camera, so that you can become more aware of how you might be perceived.

- Refer to the adult parties by their last names preceded by Mr., Mrs., Ms. or Miss. While you may comfortably refer to them by their first names outside the courtroom, it tends to sound too casual from the witness box.

- Be fair and balanced in your evidence. In the exercise of assessing your credibility as a witness, the court will be looking at many factors. The testimony of an overly rigid and opinionated witness will be quickly discounted and may inspire opposing counsel to be particularly aggressive in cross-examination. On the other hand, a balanced, thorough summary of professional contacts (and opinions if appropriate) will leave little scope for the cross-examiner.

- Take time to consider your answer, if you need it.

- Be prepared to discuss your training in and knowledge about the area in which you are testifying. For example, a social worker testifying about the circumstances surrounding disclosure by a child should be aware of methods of interviewing, the need for accurate recording and so on and should be prepared to refer to courses or training received in that area.

- If you have never testified before, it will be useful to sit in on other court proceedings before you are actually required to testify.

CROSS-EXAMINATION

As a fundamental principle of fairness, each party in a hearing has the right to test the evidence presented by the others by asking questions of their witnesses. Outside of the world of television, it is very rare for any witness to admit under cross-examination that they have lied or completely misunderstood a situation, but it is not uncommon for witnesses to qualify or limit some of the statements made in examination-in-chief.

The latitude for questioning is wide, and unlike the lawyer in direct examination, the cross-examining lawyer is free to ask leading questions, to put statements to you for your comment and generally to ask any question considered relevant to the proceedings.

If your testimony is primarily a recital of facts, then a diligent review of those facts is the best way to prepare for the witness stand.

If your opinion as an expert will be solicited, you will need to be comfortable with your assessment of a given situation and the factors that have gone into that assessment, including the facts upon which it is based. Many professionals find it useful to have colleagues role-play opposing counsel as a method of preparation.

Keep in mind the objectives of an effective cross-examination and the fact that it is *not* a personal attack.

The cross-examining lawyer may attempt to

- suggest that you may not have fully understood (or described in examination-in-chief) the context of events described in examination-in-chief;

- suggest that your perception of events may, in part, have been inaccurate or unreliable;

- explore differences between what you are saying in court and what other witnesses testified;

- explore inconsistencies between what you are saying in court and what you may have said or written on earlier occasions;

- establish that you do not have the appropriate qualifications to permit your opinions to be accorded much weight by a court;

- show that the factual basis upon which you have formed your professional assessment is incomplete, or inaccurate (e.g., you have only met one of the parties involved in a custody dispute and are relying solely upon information provided by that party);

- demonstrate that your recollection of the events in question is so poor that little weight ought to be given to your testimony or opinions;
- have you acknowledge that there are alternate, reasonable, less damaging interpretations of the facts as presented in evidence (e.g., the injuries could be accidental, caused by an ordinary fall);
- explore any ambivalence you might have about your opinion. If you have struggled in coming to your opinion about a given situation, it is not only fair but is the opposing counsel's duty to point out the aspects of your struggle that support his or her client's position. It is preferable to reveal your ambivalence in examination-in-chief;
- point out any gaps in your professional experience;
- point out that your approach to the case may have been coloured by your personal or professional biases. We all have them, and by their own definition, they are invisible to us. Colleagues can be invaluable in pointing out those issues that seem to be "hot buttons" for us.

Tips for Handling Cross-Examination

- Set the appropriate tone, by giving evidence fairly and in a balanced way during your examination-in-chief.
- Try very hard to avoid becoming angry or argumentative. Sometimes the counsel conducting a cross-examination will (intentionally or otherwise) ask questions that impugn the character, integrity or honesty of a witness. Even in this situation, the witness who reacts angrily, especially a professional, undermines his or her credibility.
- Be familiar with the interpretation of the case from the cross-examining counsel's point of view.
- Readily admit what is true, even if it doesn't particularly support your conclusion.
- If you do not remember something, candidly admit this. Never say you are sure if you are only guessing.

- Don't be trapped into a "yes" or "no" answer if that answer will potentially mislead the court. If the counsel cuts you off before you have finished, request an opportunity to complete your answer.
- If you do not understand a question, ask that it be repeated or rephrased. If it contains more than one question, break it up into manageable parts. Your answer to one question when two have been asked may not give the court a clear understanding of your evidence.
- Take a moment to consider your answer if you need it.
- Anticipate and rehearse in your own mind how you will handle personal questions or an embarrassing aspect of your professional handling of the case. (If you have made a serious error that might constitute some form of negligence or malpractice, we suggest you discuss it with a lawyer beforehand.)

TESTIFYING AS AN EXPERT

Often doctors, psychiatrists, psychologists or specially trained or experienced social workers will be asked to offer expert opinion on issues before the court. The concept of the "expert" witness was first developed in the English legal system. From its inception, the use of experts was confined to areas of special knowledge, where it was believed that a jury of citizens was incapable of interpreting the evidence without assistance. (See also "Opinion Evidence," page 85, in Chapter 5.)

The basic approach of the courts to the use of expert evidence has remained pretty much the same, although new areas of expertise are continually developing. The law does not necessarily require that expertise be obtained through formal education or professional certification. The expertise can be derived from education, experience or even a special interest unrelated to earning a living, such as a hobby. How the person acquires the specialized knowledge is secondary to the fact that it is acquired. In practice, however, the courts seem to prefer credentials related to formal education, coupled with a solid background of experience.

The following are questions people sometimes ask about testifying as an expert.

Why Testify as an Expert?

Only a witness qualified as an "expert" is entitled to offer "opinion" evidence. Normally a witness can only testify as to direct observations and cannot offer an interpretation of the events observed. For example, a social worker could say she saw bruises and proceed to describe their size, location and coloration. It is usually necessary, however, for a medical doctor to give expert evidence to offer an opinion that the bruises are inconsistent with the explanation offered by a caregiver.

If your professional opinion is to be offered to the court, your professional expertise will likely have to be established at the outset of your testimony.

In addition to being able to offer opinion evidence, the expert is entitled to refer to information that would otherwise be excluded as hearsay. The information upon which you rely for forming your opinion, however, may have to be formally proven in evidence at some point in the trial in order to establish the basis for your offered opinion. For example, if a psychiatrist has assessed a parent as being a substantial risk to a child, based at least in part upon a prior history of abusive conduct towards a spouse, it may be incumbent on the lawyer relying on that opinion to establish that history of abuse through other evidence in order to enhance the weight of that opinion.

If you are ruled an expert by the judge, you are also entitled to comment upon hypothetical fact situations. Normally a witness, even an expert witness, will be commenting on a situation with which he or she is personally familiar. Occasionally, however, an acknowledged expert in the field will be called upon to comment on the case despite the fact that he or she has had no direct contact with the parties. In this case, the facts of the case before the court are usually put to the witness by the construction of a "hypothetical fact situation." The hypothetical can also be used in "updating" an assessor, for example, who has completed the written assessment some time before the court hearing and whose opinion might need to be adjusted or confirmed according to recent developments in the case.

What Are the Disadvantages of Testifying as an Expert?

One aspect of being ruled an expert is that you can be used by opposing counsel, if they choose, in support of their own case. If, for example, you have been established as an expert in the area of sexual abuse of children, you might be questioned as to trends in the literature that undermine the theoretical approach you or another witness has taken. You might be questioned at length about the incidence of false allegations in the context of custody and access disputes. Counsel may try to embarrass you by referring to quotations from leading authorities that counter the opinion you have ventured and ask for your comment. It is wise to be in a position not only to refer to those leading authorities who are supportive of your interpretation of the facts but to point out the limitations of those authorities who undermine your approach.

Another disadvantage of testifying as an expert is the fact that preparation and a court appearance can take a great deal of time out of a busy professional schedule, frequently for compensation that is less than fully adequate.

How Am I "Qualified" as an Expert?

Some judges take a fairly informal approach to the qualification of witnesses, at least in civil cases involving the welfare of a child. They invite opinions from a variety of witnesses and attach varying weight to such opinions, depending on the witness's experience and education. You should, however, be prepared for the possibility of a more formal approach, especially in a trial.

Normally the lawyer who has called you as a witness will attempt to have you qualified as an expert at the outset of your testimony. The court needs to know

- your formal education;
- whether or not you have testified elsewhere as an expert;
- your professional experience;

- your areas of expertise;
- any research, publications or seminars you have conducted.

If you have prepared a summary of your relevant training and experience for your lawyer in advance, you may only be called upon to agree modestly as the lawyer puts the highlights of your summary to you for confirmation. This is usually the most comfortable method for witnesses. If you are called upon to detail your own qualifications, do not be overly modest. Ensure that the court knows the breadth of experience and education that you bring to your considered opinion.

Following a review of your qualifications, the lawyer will often be asked to specify for the court the area(s) of expertise for which your opinion will be offered. This requires some thought in advance of the hearing. Do you wish to be qualified as an expert in a narrow field, or do you wish to offer your opinions on a wider range of topics?

Opposing counsel are usually given an opportunity to question you concerning the specifics of your training and experience in an attempt to challenge, if appropriate, your qualifications to offer an expert opinion in the areas identified by the lawyer who called you.

Following this procedure, the judge will usually make a ruling either accepting, rejecting or qualifying the nature of expert evidence that will be received from you.

Cautions for the Expert Witness

- Do not stray from your own area of expertise into another discipline. For example, medical diagnoses cannot come from a social worker.
- Avoid using jargon. If you must use a technical term of your discipline, follow it immediately with a clear lay definition so that your testimony is understandable for all.
- Make your testimony rich with examples so that you can lead the court logically to the conclusions you have reached. Do not ask the court simply to accept your conclusions because you are the expert. Demonstrate the process you

have gone through in formulating your opinion by providing the information derived from your observations and from other sources and your analysis of that information.

- Prepare yourself for testifying as an expert by ensuring that you are familiar with the recent literature on the subject you will be testifying about.

There is some controversy about the expertise attributable to social workers. Depending on the issues before the court, many judges are willing to qualify social workers with extensive training and experience as experts in issues related to their work. Other judges seem more reluctant to acknowledge social workers as experts. Certainly most social workers will not feel qualified to offer expert opinion early in their careers. With training and experience, however, a social worker may become more qualified and comfortable in offering expert opinion evidence to the court.

QUESTIONS ABOUT TESTIFYING

Witnesses often ask the following questions about testifying.

What happens if I don't respond to a subpoena by coming to court?

If you have not made special arrangements with the lawyer who arranged for the summons or subpoena, you may be subjecting yourself to serious penalties. In a criminal case, a Crown Attorney or defence lawyer may seek a "material witness" warrant, and where you have been subpoenaed and you fail to appear, the court may issue a warrant for your arrest. In civil proceedings, your failure to appear may also lead to consequences up to and including arrest. It is therefore important to talk directly to the lawyer who has arranged for your subpoena or summons if you have a particular difficulty with attendance on the day specified on the subpoena or summons so that, if possible, another time can be arranged.

If the subpoena states a time, for example, 10.00 a.m., do I have to be at court right at that time?

If you are wondering what time you are required at court, it is best to double check with the lawyer who is calling you as his or her witness. If you are testifying in a criminal matter on behalf of the Crown, the investigating officer or Crown Attorney may be able to confirm the time you are required. It may be that you will be told to come somewhat later than your subpoena or summons indicates as the time on the document usually refers to the time of the start of the hearing and not the time that a specific witness is likely to testify. If you cannot get direct confirmation from the lawyer or police officer who has arranged for your subpoena or summons, however, you must be at court at the time indicated on the subpoena or summons.

What if I am unable to appear on the day I am supposed to testify?

If you know in advance that the date you are subpoenaed will be a problem for you, call the lawyer who has arranged for the subpoena to see if a more convenient time can be arranged. If you wake up physically ill the morning of court and are unable to testify, you should call the court directly and leave a message advising the reason for your absence and where you can be reached if it is necessary to arrange a new date. It may be best to direct your message to the lawyer who has requested you to testify.

If I have previously given a statement to the police, can I review it before I testify?

By all means. If the police officer or Crown Attorney does not provide it for you, ask for it. You can also review a transcript of your prior evidence (if it has been prepared) if you are asked to testify on more than one occasion about the same case.

What if the judge asks me a question?

Occasionally the judge will wish to ask questions of the witness that have not been asked by counsel. You are expected to answer honestly and to the best of your ability. You should not feel obliged to agree with a thesis or suggestion just because it comes from the judge. It is customary for the judge to give the other lawyers an opportunity to ask further questions that may have arisen as a result of his or her questions.

Can I sit in on the proceedings before I testify?

Often one or both of the parties will request an order excluding witnesses from being in the courtroom until the witness has completed his or her testimony. The purpose of such an order is to ensure that the testimony of the witness is not influenced or "contaminated" by hearing the testimony of others. Usually a witness is permitted to remain inside the courtroom *after* testifying. Occasionally a witness who is being asked to give expert evidence will be asked to sit in on other evidence or be exempted from an order excluding witnesses. If you have any questions about this, check with the lawyer who has called you as a witness.

If I am not comfortable swearing on the Bible, what do I do?

Each witness has the option of either swearing or affirming. An oath means swearing to tell the truth on the Bible or other Holy Book. If you do not wish to swear an oath, you may request to affirm, or make a solemn promise to tell the truth, instead. These are identical in legal effect.

Can the cross-examining lawyer look at my notes?

Yes. The lawyer is permitted to review any document that is filed in evidence and any notes to which you refer while giving evidence. In addition, if you used documents to prepare yourself for testifying, even if you did not use them on the witness stand, cross-examining counsel may ask to see them.

Can the cross-examining lawyer ask me questions about my personal life?

It is unusual but not unheard of for a professional witness to be asked personal questions while testifying. If the answer will enhance your credibility (e.g., "Ms. X., do you have any children?" "Yes, five."), and you are comfortable answering, by all means do so. If the question is not relevant or comfortable for you to answer, and if the lawyer who called you as a witness does not object to the question, turn politely to the judge and ask if an answer to the question is relevant to the proceedings.

The important thing to avoid is the appearance of defensiveness, which will be unquestionably exploited by the cross-examining lawyer to undermine your credibility. Some questions may seem to be of a personal nature, but may in fact be very relevant from a defence or judicial standpoint (e.g., "Mrs. X., you and my client have really never gotten along well, isn't that true?"). For these questions, which are legitimate material for cross-examination, a little forethought is helpful as is a lot of poise.

Should I be embarrassed about the fact that I may have discussed the case with the lawyer who has called me as a witness in the trial?

Witnesses are sometimes asked during cross-examination whether they have gone over their evidence with anyone prior to the trial. It is important to answer honestly if this type of question is asked. There is generally nothing improper in meeting with a lawyer prior to trial and reviewing proposed testimony. If the case is adjourned during the cross-examination, the witness will be expected to refrain from discussing the evidence during the adjournment period with any person, including the lawyer who has called the witness.

What if I really don't want to reveal information that was given to me in confidence?

The common law has begun in recent years to recognize occasionally a "privilege" in counselling professions other than the legal profession, where public policy considerations warrant it (see "Privilege," page 86, Chapter 5). A judge would be reluctant to recognize a privilege that would serve to preclude the reception of evidence of abuse. In matters only peripherally relevant, the court might be willing to accord a "privilege" to the professional confidante.

If you are asked a question that you prefer not to answer for this reason, turn to the judge and politely ask whether you may be excused from answering the question because of your concern regarding the confidentiality of the information. If, despite your request, you are asked by the judge to answer, proceed to do so. If you are aware that this might be an issue, you might want to seek legal advice before testifying and have a lawyer available to argue in favour of a claim for privilege.

Will my testimony be interrupted?

Sometimes a witness will be asked a question that is objected to by the other counsel. A question may be objected to for the following reasons:

- The answer to the question may contain evidence controversial in its admissibility. If a jury is involved, the judge will wish to have the jury leave the room until there has been a ruling as to the admissibility of certain evidence. This is referred to as a *voir dire* or hearing within a hearing, as discussed in Chapter 5, "The Rules of Evidence," page 73.

- Counsel may argue that the evidence invited by the question is irrelevant.

- Counsel may argue that the witness is not qualified to answer the question.

- The witness may wish to refer to a document in the course of testifying that is not in evidence.

What should I do if someone objects to a question I am asked, or to a part of my answer?

Do not be alarmed if this happens. Simply wait patiently until counsel have completed their arguments and the judge has ruled.

You will then either be instructed to proceed with your answer or the question will be ruled improper. If so instructed by a judge, restrict your answer in the manner directed.

What happens if I do not finish my evidence before a lunch break or before the end of the day?

It can be very difficult to anticipate how long a witness will be on the stand. It depends on the nature of the evidence given, the number of lawyers involved and their style of cross-examination.

If you are still in the middle of your examination-in-chief when the lunch break or end of the day occurs, you are entitled to speak with the lawyer who has called you as his or her witness, but you should not discuss your evidence with any other person until you have finished testifying.

If you are in the middle of cross-examination when the break occurs, you cannot speak with anyone about the case, including the lawyer who has called you as his or her witness. It is always best to keep in mind that "justice must be seen to be done" and avoid the appearance of fraternizing with the parties or the lawyers. This is a good opportunity to take time to reflect.

If you are "bound over" or ordered to re-attend another day of trial, you are entitled to a further witness fee for each additional day in court.

What if court seems to be running late, and I have other pressing obligations?

You are perfectly entitled as a witness to advise the court that proceeding past a certain hour will cause hardship. Many witnesses, for example, must pick up children from daycare by a certain time. It is best, however, to have a back-up plan for the day you testify so that you do not feel pressured to be elsewhere.

Am I entitled to payment for my time in court?

For some professionals, an appearance in court for a case involving child abuse is considered part of their job. Public health nurses, police officers, and child protection workers are all generally accustomed to including court appearances among their scheduled duties. For these professionals, being served with a summons may be the important thing (with or without a witness fee) so that they will be protected for purposes of information sharing.

For other professionals, the day or days in court may mean real economic hardship or significant inconvenience in a professional life not generally geared to the prospect of court appearances. The rules of each court dictate the amount of money that must by law be supplied with the summons or subpoena in order to make it binding. The amount varies from province to province, and depends upon the proceeding within the province itself. It also depends upon whether the witness is being asked to recount information only or is being called as an expert witness. If you are in doubt about whether you have been paid the correct amount, you can call the court clerk's office of the court named on the summons and inquire.

The "tariff," as it is called, determines only the amount that a court will insist that a party prove has been served on a witness before taking steps to enforce a summons if a witness fails to appear. In civil cases, the tariff is used to determine the amount that a party may be required to reimburse the other if the court makes an order that "costs are payable."

In most cases where an expert is concerned, an amount above the "tariff" is usually negotiated independently between the professional and the lawyer who asks that professional to appear, based on reasonable compensation for the time of preparation and court appearance. It is important for you to discuss a fee that can be adjusted to the unpredictability of litigation, perhaps a half-day and whole day block fee arrangement.

In criminal matters, any fee discussions should be conducted with the Crown in advance. Any variation from the tariff that usually applies must be obtained by the Crown in advance of the trial.

HIGHLIGHTS OF CHAPTER 6

This chapter provided some practical suggestions for making notes for use on the witness stand and a summary that may be used in your preparation for testifying. The chapter reviewed some of the questions you may want answers to in order to have as much information as possible before you testify.

The chapter also contained some tips for giving evidence and withstanding cross-examination, and a brief commentary for those who are offering "expert" evidence.

Some of the important points to remember are:

- Notes made of specific events should be objective, thorough and made as close to the event as possible.

- If you refer to notes while testifying, you may be questioned about them, and cross-examining counsel will be permitted to review them.

- You may wish to seek legal advice about how much information to give the lawyers in advance of court.

- Even if you are not willing to share information before court, it may be wise to talk to the lawyer calling you as a witness to discuss practical issues about your court appearance unrelated to your evidence; if contacted, you should be prepared to talk to any lawyers involved in the case, as long as there are no confidentiality concerns.

- When you testify in direct examination, remember that the lawyer is limited in the kinds of questions that he or she can ask. Be fair and balanced in your testimony.

- When you are being cross-examined, remember that the lawyer is carrying out a professional duty. It is not a personal attack.

- A witness who testifies as an expert should be prepared to discuss leading authorities in the area of their expertise and to explain significant related principles.

THE IMPORTANCE OF THE COURT

The court system that we have for the purpose of resolving our social disputes is far from perfect. The formality is seen by some as intimidating and unnecessary. The delays inherent in applying notions of fairness are particularly frustrating to those who know so well the impact of delay upon the lives of children.

Despite its failings, our court system remains the method our society has chosen for resolving disputes when less formal attempts at dispute resolution have failed.

We hope the information in this book has helped you better understand some of the reasons that courtrooms function the way they do and your role as a court witness.

If you care about children and their future, you may have to become involved in the court process, even though it may be uncomfortable, unpleasant or even embarrassing. The court-room remains a major forum for making decisions about children. If you wish to play an effective role in ensuring that the rights of children are respected, you must be prepared to enter the witness box when it is in the courtroom that the determination of a child's future lies.

INDEX

Forthcoming

JUVENILE JUSTICE SYSTEMS
An International Comparison of Problems and Solutions

Edited by:

Nicholas M.C. Bala *(Queen's University)*, Joseph P. Hornick *(Canadian Research Institute for Law and the Family)*, and Howard N. Snyder *(National Center for Juvenile Justice)*
ISBN 1-55077-127-2

Despite a decrease in overall crime rates, the issues of youth crime and youth violence are a growing political and public policy concern in many countries. Policy-makers and juvenile justice officials are trying to develop more effective strategies to prevent youth crime, develop new alternatives to traditional juvenile justice systems, and find better methods for handling serious and persistent offenders.

Juvenile Justice Systems: An International Comparison of Problems and Solutions provides a detailed description and analysis of the juvenile justice systems of eight predominantly English-speaking jurisdictions with a common legal heritage: the United States, Canada, England, Scotland, Northern Ireland, the Republic of Ireland, Australia, and New Zealand. Experts from each country analyze the political and social context of youth crime in their jurisdiction, describe the rates of youth crime, and identify the policies and innovative approaches to youth justice that have been successful in their countries.

This book will be of special interest to students in criminology, social work, and law; policy-makers at various levels of government; program developers; and professionals, such as lawyers, judges, social workers, probation officers, and correctional workers who provide services in the juvenile justice system and are seeking a broader perspective on the issues they are facing.

For more information:
www.thompsonbooks.com